Say No

How to Stand Your Ground, Reclaim Your Time and Energy

(Learn the Essential High Performance Skill, Stop People Pleasing and Live Life)

Eric Killian

Published By **Zoe Lawson**

Eric Killian

All Rights Reserved

Say No: How to Stand Your Ground, Reclaim Your Time and Energy (Learn the Essential High Performance Skill, Stop People Pleasing and Live Life)

ISBN 978-1-998927-68-5

Legal & Disclaimer

The information contained in this book is not designed to replace or take the place of any form of medicine or professional medical advice. The information in this book has been provided for educational & entertainment purposes only.

The information contained in this book has been compiled from sources deemed reliable, and it is accurate to the best of the Author's knowledge; however, the Author cannot guarantee its accuracy and validity and cannot be held liable for any errors or omissions. Changes are periodically made to this book. You must consult your doctor or get professional medical advice before using any of the suggested remedies, techniques, or information in this book.

Table Of Contents

Chapter 1: Saying No Nicely to Your Family and Friends 1

Chapter 2: Saying No Nicely to Your Significant Other 17

Chapter 3: Saying No Nicely for your Boss & Co-humans 22

Chapter 4: Saying No Nicely to Social Functions 41

Chapter 5: Saying No Nicely to Yourself . 49

Chapter 6: The Art of Manipulation 52

Chapter 7: Separate Refusal from Rejection 54

Chapter 8: Learning the Ropes 56

CHAPTER 9: Learning to Say No 63

CHAPTER 10: Personal Development Through Positive Self-Motivation 102

CHAPTER 11: Optimism is Good For You 152

Chapter 1: Saying No Nicely to Your Family and Friends

"Sometimes no is the kindest phrase."

Now, this may sound a touch crazy...but I didn't recognize that you may truely say no to family and buddies. I understand, I recognise!

Let me gift the subsequent situations as they may help keep your dating on a truthful keel. Say no nicely within the following situations: For all conditions concerning renting belongings, giving or selling a car, boat, house or loaning your coins. You might also do nicely to clearly say no . . . Maximum of the time.

The motive for thinking two times about any state of affairs that consists of the transaction of cash, time and employer is that our relationships have a tendency to result in harm feelings. Our courtrooms are bursting on the seams with times that contain own family, buddies, buddies and loaning coins. If you intend to move forth with loaning coins and also you do not have a preference to mention no, ensure to have all transactions in writing and notarized. Going forward, this will shield your private home and inspire the receiver of your price range to take this transaction critically.

Invariably, your buddy asks for a loan, your cousin asks to lease your vacant property, your aunt asks you to donate to a charity. Do these requests sound acquainted? I apprehend it may be uncomfortable to flip down requests from people close to you. The herbal response is to genuinely swallow difficult and say sure to such requests, certainly to keep away from the unpleasant consequences.

The trouble is, announcing yes to such requests might also have unpleasant repercussions all on their own costing you time, money or each, pronouncing sure can also require that you do subjects no longer in step with your non-public beliefs. Have you located that at the same time as you are saying sure to certain requests, you are regularly caught in that position for lifestyles! For example, you compromise to pick out out-up the donuts for the workplace on one precise event, however due to your a success finishing touch of that mission, you have got got got now been particular because the character to select out-up the donuts, FOREVER! A smooth response which encompass, "I might be satisfied to select out out-up the donuts this week, but going ahead, we will have a time desk for the donut run".

Saying yes might also bring about similar re?uests being made in the future. In specific in the long term, saying sure can damage relationships greater than now not having stated no from the begin. For this purpose, here's how to minimize the chance of damage feelings or a damaged relationship when you must reject a request.

Don't offer a direct solution

It may need to appear, a pal or relative can be especially insulted by a short rejection as it sends the message that you didn't take the time to consider the re?uest, deeming it unworthy of consideration. If they request an instantaneous reaction, ask for a few minutes to collect your thoughts, take a look at your calendar or even take a second to use the restroom. Why? You want to take this more time to think! If you offer yourself this an lousy lot wished time, even a second or , you're giving your self valuable moments to respire, think and mirror.

Although you could in the end say no nicely, the man or woman receiving the solution will understand which you as a minimum gave your no response some real idea. Some humans locate it so tough to say no to friends or own family that their no's come out as a perhaps or maybe a certain. Presumably, probable way positive because of the truth the individual making the request will suppose, "Well, you in no way in truth stated no!". In this case, when the time comes to give your answer, be smooth from the onset that you're announcing no. Look the individual in the attention, don't snicker, don't smile or make light of the request. Be forthright, honest, kind, and sincere. Think approximately how you will sense if someone is telling you, no.

The same regulations observe if you are at the smartphone or sending a textual content or electronic mail. You can enjoy the tone of the texts and emails however the truth that you don't see the character.

Express gratitude

Remind your self that the person wouldn't have asked in the event that they didn't experience close enough to accept as true with you. Follow up your clear rejection by expressing gratitude for that closeness. Keep your response simple. If you need to say no be organisation and direct. Use phrases such as;

"It means hundreds to me that our relationship is close enough that you can come to me with this request. I'm really sorry I can't come through for you."

"Thanks for coming to me, but I'm afraid it's now not reachable right now." "I'm sorry, but I can't help this night time."

"Thank you for asking, however my plate is overflowing proper now, and this isn't a excellent time for me!"

"Thank you for taking into account me, I simply do understand it, however this is not an tremendous time for me!

This is my desired response and right right here's why; even as you reply with a response, much like the above example, all and sundry feels right because of the reality the person making the request has been heard and you've got got stated no with out ever the use of the phrase no.

Explain your motives

If possible, provide a brief explanation for the rejection—one that does not mirror terrible on the individual making the re?uest. If you select to offer an purpose in the back of your answer, maintain in mind that that may be a preference and now not a need. Explain that the re?uest does now not in shape a system you have in place or policies you must follow. This makes the rejection seem less non-public.

Keep in thoughts, that human beings usually do no longer get maintain of no's well. Especially from the choice makers, the "move-to" people. Every family, each friendship has someone who they depend on to get topics executed. If you are that character, it would behove you to steadily take steps to lessen their reliance and dependence on you.

Why is that this important? Well, due to the fact you've got got a life and also you want to live it and revel in it...You can absolutely need to get rid of a few topics from your plate.

Training humans to definitely be given your no

There are folks who might also allow you to understand -- not ask you -- to do something. Keep in thoughts, you are now education them to understand your no's. This can take a hint time. Be affected man or woman during this transition because because of your facts of announcing sure, you have got were given unknowingly expert people to count on a sure answer!

Generally, we're all educated to do nice matters. For example, you wake-up and go to artwork at a certain time. You may additionally strength or take a educate at a high-quality time as nicely. Training is something we're all particularly familiar with, whether or now not consciously or unconsciously. When you begin pronouncing no properly, you will likely get some push-returned as in guilt-trips. People may additionally moreover additionally marvel; are you feeling well? Did you and your massive different have an difficulty? What's the trouble? Remember, that is the manner you've educated them to be! So be information, however don't trade your no to a sure. Stick for your guns! The desire to mention no need to begin somewhere, and that somewhere is now!

You shouldn't wait till a wedding, commencement, (Or any large occasion) to start retraining. It's tremendous to start small, likely a assembly or luncheon, and circulate up at the identical time as crucial. Are you afraid? I advise are you scared to demise to say no nicely or say no in any respect? Unconsciously you have determined that it's higher to be in all people's correct graces than to stand up for yourself. I get it! You certainly might want to invite yourself why? Why is it so critical for me to revel in desired, subsequently used and normally abused? Only you could answer that question. This ebook is proper proper here to offer you some gear, but they will be not the give up-all-be-all, and that they advocate now not some thing if you don't pick out out to use them.

Don't revel in accountable for saying no to your children

It is vital for a kid to pay interest no from time to time, in order that they growth a feel of power of will. Navigating adult lifestyles without this critical skills is hard. Rather than cave into their protests, let them know who is in charge through the usage of putting boundaries.

There will come a time at the same time as you will say no and located a caveat...while your room is clean, (Dishes washed, vehicle washed, garden mowed and so on.), you could do...

To be quite honest, kids recognize boundaries. They can also by no means let you know, however they need a person to be on pinnacle of things, particularly while the limits are clean and concise.

Nice nos for Mom or Dad

Have you ever stated effective for your dad and mom on the equal time as you knew for your coronary heart you need to have said no? I assume all of us have. How can I say no at the same time as my parents gave me lifestyles, changed my diapers, helped me with my homework and sacrificed for me. Who virtually desires to say no to Mom or Dad?

For some, the problem of pronouncing no to their dad and mom stems from the inevitable feelings of guilt that follows. People are inclined to assist their mother and father because of the truth as a little one (Even these days), their dad and mom generally helped them. But try and observe it this way; whilst you have been a baby it changed into your discern's obligation to decide what modified into top or awful for you. On occasion, your dad and mom made options for you that during all possibility precipitated them to sense accountable, but it emerge as the right desire to your nicely-being. Today it's miles your obligation to make the right alternatives for your self. Naturally, you'll experience accountable for saying no in your mother and father, but like your dad and mom, you cannot allow the feeling of guilt to decide what's pleasant for you!

Saying sure to a later date

Another way to say no is thru postponing the request. Timing is the whole thing and on occasion you might be asked to do something even as you are right inside the middle of a more vital venture. Don't hesitate to say that you are worried in a undertaking right now, but possibly you may be to be had to assist at a later date or time.

However, you ought to by no means provide to do something inside the destiny if you don't clearly suggest it. This may additionally moreover want to emerge as masses worse than simply having stated no in the first place. Usually we need to check our schedules in advance than we can make any strength of mind, a smooth "Let me get lower lower back to you", could make all the difference.

Keep in mind, it's not a brilliant idea to say this when you mean no within the first place. This will waste their time that might have been better spent finding someone else, who could've gladly said yes.

Saying no with love . . .

Even even though, we by no means want to disappoint cherished ones, the worry we might also moreover have with parents is that they will come what might also prevent loving us if we're saying no to a request. That isn't always true, but what is real is that the priority of losing love and elegance actions you to mention yes while there are times you really want to say no.

The equal idea applies in conjunction with your extended circle of relatives and pals. Be sincere, type, sincere, but say no. Project power to your body language and don't over-apologize. This doesn't suggest which you have to look suggest or disillusioned at the same time as you say no. You simplest need to be respectful.

The tone of your voice is in particular crucial. Although you will be overworked and crushed earlier than you talk take three-breaths and accumulate your mind. Though it could feel like an eternity, in the long run it is going to be properly worth it.

The electricity of this method is speakme with sincerity and clarity. Although saying no isn't continuously clean, with exercise you will grow on this vicinity.

Worksheet

When have you ever ever ever stated superb on the identical time as you desired to say no?

Chapter 2: Saying No Nicely to Your Significant Other

"Saying no can be the very last self-care."

Knowing how to set appropriate boundaries also can furthermore make the difference in whether or no longer your relationship succeeds.

Your massive unique expresses a fantastic deal emotional drama requiring an excessive amount of hobby, you may additionally moreover need to discover ways to set limits by way of using the use of saying no. Learning the way to say no is not necessarily easy however may be essential to avoid uncomfortable situations.

If a direct question is requested, be polite, and say "I'm so sorry, however I can't." If that's too difficult, say you ought to test with a person or a few aspect else (Your calendar, your children, your Mom, Dad, your boss, or your buddy) or assume about it before you answer. You also can get a guilt journey, however you never apprehend, you can no longer.

Watch on TV and in movies for examples of people saying no with grace and compassion (You can find them if you look). How do they're announcing no properly? What is their tone? Is it impartial, immoderate pitched or low pitched? Are they yelling? Where are their eyes at the same time as they're addressing the opportunity individual with a no? Do they face the character or do their eyes marvel? Your body language is a enormous thing even as you're saying no. Do your lips say no, but your body says sure? A flirty demeanor, excessive laughter or smiling sends mixed messages hard the individual receiving the facts.

We can, at instances, be our very very own worst enemy. We say one aspect and imply every different (Many humans had been accountable of that). You want to make your sure imply sure and your no mean no. The lofty and insincere sure and the wishy-washy and susceptible no aren't accurate for absolutely everyone. They display a lack of understand for your self and for the character making the request. I as speedy as overheard a conversation wherein a gentleman said, "Why didn't he genuinely say no from the start and we may want to have avoided this massive waste of time?" Due to the alternative birthday party's lack of ability to speak a clean and concise no, that gentleman professional a systemic societal problem, money and time were out of place!

You don't want to say no, all of the time! If you're making it a addiction of saying no to the entirety that comes your way, the invites will forestall coming. A rule of thumb is: if you say no to three invitations in a row (To the identical person or the same or similar event), you may be eliminated from the listing of invitees. So, use warning as you're pronouncing no to avoid being eliminated from the visitor list.

Worksheet

Why will you say no on your sizeable other?

_____

_____

_____

_____

_____

_____

_____

_____

_____

____

How will you are saying no?

_____

_____

_____

_____

_____

_____

_____

_____

_____

____

When is the extraordinary time to mention no?

_____

_____

_____

_____

_____

_____

_____

_____

_____

____

Chapter 3: Saying No Nicely for your Boss & Co-humans

"Half of the problems of this life may be traced to announcing certain too rapid and not announcing no fast sufficient."

It isn't always what you are saying, however the way you say it...

You've were given too many stuff on your plate, the assignments keep coming, you're being requested to work each different weekend in a row and there's no way you could sit thru a few special team dinner after a long day on the office. Everyone ultimately hits a breaking point.

While on the other hand, the concept of saying no to your boss has your knees shaking. This is likely new territory for you, so here are some pointers to not best get the task done, but sincerely as vital, live on your bosses good side.

Be Rational

Many times, the first step to saying no is to do away with many false assumptions on your part. The first being fear, due to the reality fear of reprisal keeps one from ever status up for themselves. Ask yourself, "What's the worst thing that can likely take region if I say no? Keep in mind, it is not what you're pronouncing, however how you say it! You'll be surprised that the solution probably isn't as bad as you might imagine, and the benefits almost always outweigh the risks.

Given all this, it's far super that you do no longer say no on the equal time as surrounded with the aid of way of others, if possible. Why is that this? It's better to hold the no to a communication amongst you and your boss, as you don't want to come across as someone who's being insubordinate or now not a collection player. Additionally, the no you want to deliver can be some thing that everybody must not be privileged to pay interest.

Usually while one is speakme to someone in a feature of authority, the humans spherical are taking look at. They are figuring out how they'll technique the boss at the same time as the time comes for his or her want to say no, and that point will in truth arrive in the end.

Your boss has a boss and also you want to get your task accomplished and do it well, but there will come a time while you ought to mention no... Well.

Start early

When dealing with what is probably an ungainly scenario, do no longer wait to push another time till you've hit your breaking point even as feelings may be at a fever pitch. By "blowing up" you'll run the risk of looking like a loopy person if you wait until you're crushed. You need to begin drawing boundaries as soon as you start your manner. The aim is to usually protect it gradual.

But other than that, saying no on your boss may be scary in case you're not accustomed to it. At a few point, the time will come for you to take a step outside of your comfort zone to safeguard your sanity. No one else will do it for you, but you want to hold your pastime, so tread on this shape of manner that you'll usually be held inside the highest esteem and revered.

On one occasion once I informed my boss no, the manage made me pay for it via using punitive measures to make my interest depressing. I have been categorized because of the reality the sure man or woman and my boss relied on my positive. I had professional all people in my international to depend on me and the surprise of the no became disruptive to their mindset of me due to the truth I sooner or later stood up for myself.

I waited completely too lengthy to mention no. I should have started out out sooner with small nos' and then the expectation ought to have not been there for a assured yes.

Be remarkable to ease into this new you via taking small steps! Be affected person due to the fact commonly humans do no longer like change and, certain, that includes you! Don't really leap in and begin saying no to every request, while definitely ultimate week you've got been the certain person.

Keep in thoughts that your no might not be acquired nicely, relying on your fame in the administrative center. The feature you hold certainly topics and can be instrumental to your potential to mention no nicely.

Receiving a nice no

I obtained the nicest no from a CEO of a non-profits. My husband and I are with a network advertising employer and in the route of a cellphone appointment with a gentleman, he stated, "Tell me, how can I be of service to you?" I proceeded to offer an cause behind all the benefits our corporation furnished and the way the proceeds need to fund scholarships for his non-profits business enterprise. The gentleman listened and then said, "You sound very well versed approximately your product, but inside the interim, we aren't worried". What a manner to say no nicely. He in no way used the phrase no in his response. What I undergo in thoughts about that come across changed into truly how remarkable the no become. He have become so type, considerate and sincere. To be quite sincere, as quickly as I say no, I try to emulate this gentleman in his demeanor, speech and inflection. I anticipate my appreciation stems from the reality that he permit me inform my tale first earlier than announcing no.

Propose alternatives

However, if you have a boss who might be less than receptive, throw an alternative solution on the table. It shows that you're inclined to paintings with them and starts a speak around options. For example, "I am not available to work late this week, however I am to be had to art work late next week".

Buy yourself some time. Interrupt the positive cycle, using phrases like "I'll get back to you," then consider your alternatives. Having idea it thru at your leisure, you'll be capable of say no with greater self guarantee.

Ask Questions

In the administrative center we have a propensity to assume every request is mandatory... However are they? Considered asking if this mission can be completed later date or time? You may want to likely enlist a co-employee to help you to prioritize your to-do list or discover help to get everything done. Bosses are human and sometimes they need a chunk help seeing opportunity solutions.

No one want to word

You don't want to make this some factor that becomes the communicate of the place of work. If you're saying no properly efficiently, no person should also be aware but you'll realise the difference and that's what topics.

If someone does phrase, it can sound some detail like; "I determined that you usually volunteer for such-and-such, but your call have become not on the listing...What's happening?" The manager may also test to see if the whole thing is ok with you; "We have been involved approximately you due to the fact we have been searching ahead to going for walks with you on that mission, software, and plenty of others."

Although you're making modifications on your lifestyles, it is better to chorus from pronouncing the modifications you are making. If it will become tremendous which you are no longer the certain individual...Then you virtually are announcing no incorrectly.

Focus on the impact

Ever notice that when someone explains why they're saying no it usually softens the blow? Your boss is no different. Your boss cares about you, however they really care approximately the industrial commercial enterprise organization desires. If there is a manner to connect the dots and show the boss why saying no nicely will yield better results, or keep away from awful ones, do it. For instance, "I am targeted on the subsequent debts and giving the purchaser my undivided interest".

Choose your battles

While you don't want to be a yes individual, you don't want to always cry wolf. Make sure when you say no, you're doing so for a good cause, not just to be tough. When the time comes and you do take a stand, human beings will respect you for it.

Saying No Nicely to Co-human beings

"Half of the issues of this existence can be traced to pronouncing positive too speedy and now not saying no soon sufficient."

-Josh Billings

Do you often discover yourself saying yes to re[?]uests at work? Requests for time that always seem to call for your interest - through cellular phone, email, right away messages, meetings, or in person. Do you always have a hard time saying no?

I understand your apprehensions about announcing no, as it can disappoint the individual to whom you're saying no to. If you apprehend or hope that you will be walking with that person in the future, you'll want to continue to have a good relationship with them and saying no can also jeopardize that courting. By declining a request can you may be perceived as uncooperative and nobody wants to be perceived in a terrible manner.

So, right here's another way of looking at things. To stay green and minimize strain, you have to learn the art of the way to say no nicely in your co-people. If you have a problem saying no, you're not alone. Many people find it very difficult to refuse requests, especially underneath the stress of the paintings place settings.

There is a fashionable agreement that you may in no manner be productive if you take on too many commitments - you simply spread yourself too skinny! If you typically say sure to the whole thing that is asked of you, you may not always be capable of get some factor executed, at least no longer nicely or on time. Know your priorities and rate your time.

Perhaps the maximum vital detail is: What are your priorities and the way precious is time for you? Consider this for a moment...While a co-worker asks you to dedicate some of your time to something, and you know deep down that you simply have hundreds on your plate, be firm enough to say that your plate is overloaded with different priorities. However, there are numerous techniques so one may be used as a manner to steer you to mention yes.

- But you said no remaining week.

- You are not being a team participant.

- Some people expect you are losing your location.

- Don't you need that advertising and marketing and marketing

- So-and-so said that you haven't been as involved as you as soon as were.

Remember, despite the fact that you do have a chunk extra time, you're looking for and promoting this in exchange for time with more pressing matters at work or with your family and friends.

Apologies can now and again weaken the no

To somewhat lessen our guilt, we often say sorry when we say no because it sounds greater well mannered. While agreed that politeness is important, sometimes apologizing an excessive amount of can make your no sound weak. Understand when you need to sound unapologetic approximately guarding your time and priorities. Remember: Be sincere, type, respectful and be wonderful . . . However, say no.

Recently, you have been requested to join the commercial enterprise company volleyball crew. You played volleyball in college, however you were now not specifically top at it. The group desires one greater player and you've got been requested via numerous co-human beings to sign up for. What do you do? Do you are pronouncing, yes or do you're saying no properly? Keeping in thoughts which you already are overworked and burdened out. Saying no will come up with a few aspect that you don't have right now...Time!

This is not to mention that pronouncing no may be easy. It will no longer be easy! Many extremely good relationships are made within the direction of a bonding time together with sports activities sports. I do now not need to dissuade you from taking element in any hobby which you find out exciting. To the opposite! Saying no will open alternatives for you, in which you may have time while you aren't overworked.

You can say, "Let me reflect onconsideration on it and I'll get returned to you". If you recognize for nice that gambling volleyball (Or any sport for that rely variety) is not something that you need to revisit, pronouncing no nicely is constantly the better solution.

When it's difficult to say no or you're unsure if you can take on the re?uest, tell the person "I will supply your re?uest some concept and get decrease again to you with the aid of day after today". This is a good way to assist you to give it some hobby, and double-check your priorities and commitments. Explain that you need to be allotted the proper amount of time to make the great desire. This can be intricate because the man or woman might also moreover say some aspect like; "Well the undertaking isn't due for 90-days, that need to offer you with time to come lower back back onboard and make contributions." The reason of the announcement is to steer you which you'll have good enough time.

This is why announcing no nicely is the better solution. Saying no leaves no wiggle room for a person to interject with possibility plans, times, and places that might otherwise appoint your capabilities and abilities.

Make your first answer no...

During those sports while a right away answer is vital, it's miles higher to err at the element of warning and say no well. It is much less hard to exchange your no to a sure than it's miles to exchange a positive to a no! Once you decide to taking a person's shift, if you could't paintings that shift, guess who is now liable for finding a alternative? But, if you say no nicely proper from the beginning, the individual desiring the insurance will have to get someone else to cover the shift...You'll now not be accountable! You do now not should get concerned. Yeah! It kinda takes the stress off.

Understand the effects

There is the argument that human beings might also moreover try to retaliate in opposition to you for announcing no nicely. They can also moreover save you talking to you, received't take your shifts or say no to some component you request within the future. I'm now not saying this can occur, I'm pronouncing this could show up.

What do you do if this happens to you? You deal with it! You can ask a person else. This is why it is so important to be kind and say no properly but firmly.

Try to practice the following body language if you don't want to be perceived as being prone.

1. Stop what you're doing and face the individual making the request.

It will take about 1-2 seconds to offer your standard and whole attention. No cell cellphone. No laptop. Give the person your undivided interest.

2. Maintain eye contact.

As this can affect the impact of your words and your capacity to say no. Treat human beings consisting of you want to be dealt with and you could now not go wrong at the same time as you say no properly.

3. Refrain from immoderate smiling or giggling.

I cannot explicit this enough. Smiling or giggling can purpose people to no longer take you or your no seriously. You do now not need to be suggest or aggressive. Simply chorus from smiling and laughter in case you need your no to be perceived as excessive.

Worksheet

Can you're saying no on your boss/co-humans?

Chapter 4: Saying No Nicely to Social Functions

"You can be an first rate character with a type coronary coronary heart and although say no."

A request can are available many paperwork. Let's say you get hold of an invite through snail mail. Now that you understand the power of pronouncing no, it's exceptional to say no the invite in the same fashion that it became furnished to you. This form of etiquette applies in every degree of verbal exchange (Telephone, text, emails and in man or woman). Give the inquiring for birthday party the equal admire that grow to be given to you.

In a family, friends or institution of affiliates, there's continuously an upcoming occasion. Whether it's a birthday, barbecue, picnic or get-together. It's normal to enjoy social features and have amusing together.

Regardless of the event, probable you've already made plans. You need to go to a piece-associated event otherwise you've been invited somewhere, and you're expected to reveal up. Whatever it's miles, it's no longer constantly a lousy element to cancel plans. As lots as you'd want to be best, you aren't perfect and sometimes you actually need to offer yourself a spoil and say no. Remember, you do no longer need to make a dependancy of announcing sure and constantly reversing the answer, even if you are pronouncing no properly.

Depending on the obligation, you might also furthermore want to offer as few data as feasible. It's your time and if you feel like the alternative party doesn't need to realise why you can't make it, then limit what you say.

At times, actual-existence issues come up that aren't for others to know. Explain that you have a non-public emergency or express which you're handling greater pressing issues within the mean time. Being honest is top, but you pleasant have to be as open as you need. If they respect you, they'll respect your need for privacy. Try to be sincere to the possibility party and mean it (Even if it's a few element—or someone—you dislike).

If you express regret for withdrawing, make the effort to reschedule plans as soon as possible (Depending at the situations). Since you recuse your self from something you don't have any desire to do, you could store face by showing some interest. Keep subjects open with phrases like, "Maybe we can reschedule sometime soon?" or "I'll get back to you once I have time to attempt again." If you do want to reschedule, that's even better! If you have not any plans to reschedule or the occasion cannot be rescheduled, it behoves you to ask approximately the event. Example: "I am so sorry I couldn't make the assembly, dinner, or celebration, thru the manner, how become it?" Here is in which a few human beings make the mistake and say that it's far adequate to inform "a piece white lie", along side, "I modified into unwell, I had a immoderate fever." Anything to get out of the event. Do you notice that announcing no properly proper from the start could have been greater suitable? Just do not interact inside the act of lying. "When you inform a lie, you'll usually need to consider the lie you knowledgeable...at the same time as you tell the reality, it sits there huge and ambitious."

Saying no nicely can also sound like a horrible idea, however in the end, saying no can be at times an exquisite concept!

In our domestic, we cope with social features based totally totally totally on which event we have been invited to first. This rule has been beneficial on the equal time as receiving multiple invitations for awesome activities hung on the equal day. I simply have said, "Thank you for contemplating us, however we've got a previous dedication."

There were times I in reality have stated, "Maybe we will come the subsequent time," which softens the reaction. Remember, you may't do everything or be the whole thing to all and sundry. Invitations to social occasions can are to be had many paperwork. Some are merely, "Save the Date", notifications and others require a organization RSVP. When you are pronouncing no, recognize they may be trying to plot for the occasion and your no can be taken into consideration definitive. It have to be unusual a good way to ask to change your no right proper into a certain later. You may ask, "Why should I ever need to do this?" Well, for starters, matters alternate! If your no can become a certain and you've for my part contacted the host/hostess to inquire if there may be room for you and a vacationer. Why? Because topics alternate! If you don't experience comfortable or you believe you studied that it's too overdue, you can in no manner realise till you ask.

Case-in-point, we were invited to a huge circle of relatives birthday party on the identical date of a marriage. The bridal ceremony "Save-the-Date" assertion came even as we showed the party. The birthday woman changed into ill, and the birthday celebration have emerge as rescheduled.

At first, I became uncomfortable contacting the bride to allow her recognise that our plans had changed on such brief note. I did name and described what occurred at the final minute. I confronted my pain and wager what? Two of her out-of-town website online visitors had truly cancelled and my husband and I had been capable of attend the marriage. Things do exchange, they absolutely do!

Worksheet

When do you observed you may want to mention no to a unique occasion?

_____

_____

_____

_____

_____

_____

_____

_____

____

Why do you think you may want to mention no?

_____

_____

_____

_____

_____

_____

_____

_____

_____

___

How will you're announcing no?

_____

_____

_____

_____

_____

_____

_____

_____

_____

___

Chapter 5: Saying No Nicely to Yourself

"To thine private self be actual."

On severa events, overspending, overeating and over-eating, are instances in which announcing no to your self might be the hardest no you could ever say, due to the truth there is no obligation, and no witnesses...Just you!

I have to admit, once I say no to myself, and I don't consume the whole slice of pie, and as an opportunity, devour one-1/2 of of it, I experience in reality proper approximately myself and my self guarantee goes up a notch. These victories, however small they may seem, come to be big wins in the ordinary photograph of our lives. Each time you are saying no to yourself, you are developing and maturing in saying no. You had been kind to your self, an awesome manner to most effective assist you to be kinder to others. Indirectly, empathy will train you the proper way to say no to a person else. When you are pronouncing no nicely to yourself, you also are saying sure to something extra vital to you.

Worksheet

When will you need to say no to your self?

_____

_____

_____

_____

_____

_____

_____

_____

_____

____

How will you are announcing no to your self?

_____

_____

_____

_____

_____

_____

_____

_____

_____

____

Why will you assert no to your self?

_____

_____

_____

_____

_____

_____

_____

_____

____

Chapter 6: The Art of Manipulation

"The oldest, shortest phrases - "yes" and "no" are those which require the maximum concept."

If you are saying sure to a person hoping that they'll say positive to you within the future, preserve in thoughts which you are education the art work of manipulation. You are not saying no because you're believing (falsely) that your positive will assure you a future positive from them. I am certain that we have all finished this at one time or some different, however that doesn't make it right.

What if you say sure to a person's request and in keeping with week or later you visit that same individual to request some detail of them and that they say no on your request. How do you feel? Don't you revel in indignant? You are angry handiest because of the truth your little ploy did no longer pass the way you had deliberate. Sorry, but it occurs!

Let's take the identical state of affairs and strive coping with matters the proper way.

A positive man or woman asks you to do some thing, and this time in choice to saying sure, (In expectation that the want could be returned), to say no nicely. The amazing plan of action is to continuously be honest with the character making the request. There have become in no way a assure that they might have helped you anyway. Just because of the reality you assert sure, doesn't imply certain may be stated back to you!

Chapter 7: Separate Refusal from Rejection

"I do no longer take transport of as real with in turning down people, surely the topics they request."

Usually, human beings will understand that it is your right to say no, just as it is their right to ask the favor. Be that as it can, whilst someone says no, (Even within the occasion that they stated it properly), people commonly enjoy rejected to a degree. That is why it's so important for you to mention no nicely. Put yourself in their shoes...How might you need someone to talk to you?

Many humans do not understand the way to cut up refusal from rejection. But the manner you pick out to say no should make the distinction. It is usually exquisite to preserve your response clean in case you want to say no. Try phrases together with:

Thanks for coming to me, but I'm afraid it's not convenient right now. I'm sorry, but I can't help this midnight.

I'm sorry, however I can't assist.

Thank you for deliberating me, however my plate is overflowing right now and this isn't an notable time for me!

Unfortunately, I'm not able to take this on, but thanks for considering me.

Unfortunately, I in reality have a warfare and may't make it, however thank you for the invitation.

Whenever possible, undergo in thoughts a compromise. Only do so if you want to agree with the re□uest however keep away from compromising if you really need or need to say no well.

Chapter 8: Learning the Ropes

"No is a whole sentence and so regularly we neglect about that."

-Susan Gregg

Tip #1 – Remain Respectful

Regardless of the seize 22 state of affairs you're in, whether or not you're about to make the grandest deal of your existence for a large employer enterprise or just a nice change with a family member, you want to make a nicely-knowledgeable desire. Often, this includes having to mention NO. Remember that the one issue you could in no way get lower back is time. You can also moreover moreover declare that you're boldly giving uncertainty a danger to go into your life and probably spice matters up, but you recognise what? It's not known as taking a chance; it's virtually being silly. Rather than getting into a wholesome unprepared, be organized to play with the right gambling playing cards. The final detail you want is to fail because of your private misdoing.

The Problem of Being the Go-to

Not announcing NO makes you approachable but it could additionally make topics complex. If you bear in mind your self as a move-to or a person typically all your colleagues flip to after they want a want, you might be in an inconvenient area. In a manner, you're seen as a dependable man or woman. By the compliment, you could additionally be flattered. However, take transport of as right with is exceeded to you at the rate of your non-public goals in lifestyles. Instead of concentrated on them, a while is spent dwelling at the negotiations of others.

A circulate-to is typically:

•Less unique on the extra unique topics

- Has confined time to acquire personal goals

- Prone to make horrific judgment

- Tired maximum of the time

Why Do We Sometimes Say NO Without Really Pondering on It?

There are probably instances whilst you quite say NO. Without weighing subjects extra cautiously and in reality basing your movements on a biased nature, you finalize a desire. Mostly, you begin giving in to a thing as your purpose is to avoid warfare together along side your colleagues and moreover to stay far from hardships. Although, is it your head caution you to withstand the urge to take a chance? From such an impulsive flow into, you'll probable infer that it's your intestine telling you that intending only leads to a doomed destiny. Unless it's your desire, however, it's now not a assure that it's a clever negotiating tactic.

The Three Meanings of NO

Saying NO shows which you've set subjects immediately by means of way of way of valuing your self sufficient to absorb satisfactory the ones probabilities you whole-heartedly want protected in your path. However exceptional some proposals can be, frequently, the cause they're tossed in your direction is to tempt you. Never forget about approximately that even though there can be offers that seem to vow you advantages, you have to live devoted to a bigger cause.

The Three:

1. NO can imply honesty

By not without a doubt conforming to the expectancies of your colleagues, you talk your proper intentions. Instead of fretting about a warfare of opinions, you're greater centered on being sincere in getting your problem during. They won't like your arguments, but as you're now not expressing bogus views, the opposing ends simply choose it that way.

2.   NO can imply loyalty

If you're negotiating on the fee of simply changing the stakes, now and again you've got were given to say NO and live with the particular course. A plenty high-quality avenue can be interesting, but you need to ponder the prolonged-term outcomes. Especially in case you fee your area to start, it's a clever approach to maintain making goals through it.

three.   NO can advise recognize

Refusing to provide in to a way you're uncomfortable with includes that you're not pushing your self confidence apart. Especially in case you sense so strongly about entering into opposition to a deal, you need to draw the road somewhere among you and impressing your colleagues.

Traits of People Who Say NO

People who say NO are reward-well worth. Even if it doesn't seem like it, passing on an act of rejection genuinely calls for a remarkable deal of self guarantee. It may additionally just be a word, but now not absolutely everyone is undaunted while talking it. Relationships is probably bent if recklessness comes into play. No depend how professional you observe yourself as being, you may every so often be caught thinking about the hardships of relaying a flip down.

Admirable Traits:

1. They admit their errors.

2. They are curious.

3.   They are robust-willed.

4.   They are unafraid to be wrong.

5.   They are unafraid to expose vulnerability.

6.   They are unassuming.

7.   They not frequently are seeking for approval.

eight.   They don't compare themselves to others.

nine.   They offer credit score score wherein credit is due.

CHAPTER 9: Learning to Say No

Check out your place of work. You will find out pioneers who are harried, rushed, focused, overworked, angry, disenchanted, and copied out. Inability to delegate and attempting to attend to unsolvable troubles are two of the exceptional wellsprings of these problems. Also, learning to kingdom NO in a quiet, particular, and suitable manner is one of the first steps in having the option to employ.

1.We do not nation no for this form of large quantity of motives:

2.We want to be loved

3.We haven't any bear in mind within the exceptional character's ability to carry out the obligation four.We want to nation sure due to the truth we want to HELP

5.We do now not have the foggiest idea the manner to state no in the right way

6.We have fallen into an example of misshaped wondering, so we count on announcing no isn't right

7.We have built up a dependancy of announcing sure

8.We do no longer see the manner to hire

9.We expect maintaining others accountable is a awful detail

10. You fill in your unique cause

Learn a manner to u . S . A . No:

Saying no ought to be practiced, particularly if you have practiced being an entryway tangle for quite a while. Ouch! Was that excessively unforgiving? I needed to ensure you have got been perusing. If you aren't used to putting forward no it's going to sense outsider, ordinary, and uncomfortable. Start little and clean. Practice getting unique at small nos. Like no to the server once they inquire as to whether or not or no longer you want a beverage other than water at the café.

Or however no to your teenager after they have spent their remittance. Or but no to the night time collecting wherein the list of humans to wait consists of of the sort of massive form of folks that rub you the incorrect way. What's greater, at artwork exercise disapproving of these which you do not cope with at any rate at the start.

Your degree of ardour, or absence of it, is important in having the choice to state no efficiently.

What is the first-rate possible degree of feeling or passion? Take a stab at pronouncing no with a similar degree of love that you may make use of even as you ask, "Please pass the salt?"

Timing is important too. Sometimes a yes is more comfortable and faster. Remember that expression positive becomes a dependancy. Like some one of a kind conduct, the more you state nice, the more hard it is going to be to u . S . No.

Four Different Ways to state no:

1.No.

Sometimes sincere is right. No is a fantastically turning into response to an inquiry, for example,

"Joe, I am so overworked, and you've finished your errand at the task. Might you be able to pitch in and assist me complete mine?"

"No"(a whole lot of the time what the man or woman is pronouncing inside is: "I am getting paid a comparable repayment as you and could accumulate a similar early consummation reward as you. However, I have become too bustling shopping for on the internet to complete my artwork. What's extra, I need to computer virus out in advance of agenda for the ball activity, and you are the kind of sap you typically united states of america yes. Would you be capable of pitch in and assist me complete my venture?")

There-didn't that make it much less difficult to kingdom? "No."

2.Since a huge lot of you may discover this excessively intricate, and it feels crude in case you do not have an great association with the alternative character, how approximately we try a special way-

"I'd need to. I cannot hit do what you're requesting that I do via the Tuesday afternoon due to date you have got were given requested. Now, I may additionally probable do that for you with the resource of manner of subsequent Thursday, and I should make sure that it is probably finished with the resource of the Thursday after that. Is that proper enough? No, very a whole lot we need to walk over and test whether or not or now not Suzy should useful aid you?"

How become that? Practice, exercise, and extra practice.

Now, the following one is enormously greater hard. What fashion of you want to disapprove of your leader?

3."I'd like to Boss. I am route energized with the aid of way of this. Incredibly, we're taking this on. Now please display off to me which considered truly one in all your dreams you need me to descend the list so I can suit this in so I understand the manner to organize. Is this undertaking increasingly more critical or much less vital than challenge J? Is this challenge extra vital or less critical than project Z? What's more, which more assets are to be had to artwork in this assignment? If none, which belongings may you need me to take from great undertakings?"

Lastly:

four."Chief, I am so commenced up that we are at long remaining taking a examine this. I concur with you in this undertaking being remarkably gifted. I help the way you appeared into capacity options. I am in finished affiliation with you on the assets much like the business enterprise. I think the time-define for fruition is proper on the right tune additionally.

I would possibly want to try a certainly wonderful approach. I'd which includes you to useful useful resource me in difficult x instead of y for the following a hundred and twenty days. We will area a stake within the sand at one hundred and twenty days. If you and I aren't content fabric with generally settled upon measurements at the multi-day marker, at that element, I will hammer the brakes on and run organisation at Y. Would you be able to assist me in that?

Comprehend that model #4 above want to be carried out when you have a report of truthfulness along with your chief. This is not some factor a very good manner to paintings in case you are sparkling out of the container new on your position.

Why?

Because your manager won't have the motivation to beneficial resource you, what's extra, number one below likewise should be applied when you have a report of truthfulness collectively along with your chief.

Why?

Because severa managers may also want to do not forget which you can sand sack the challenge with the aim that you can strive your solution.

For extra credit score score exercise utilizing technique four from above in four particular strategies.

1.You cannot assist contradicting chief and help them thru the use of obliging their desire

2.You cannot assist contradicting leader and request that they help you for your picked manner

three.You concur with subordinate and assist them with the resource of obliging their preference

4.You cannot help contradicting subordinate and request that they oblige your preference

Learn to disapprove of weights that don't have an area to your shoulders. At this degree, you will have the chance to explicit positive to gambling in the downpour along side your kids. You could have the hazard to specific superb to analyzing Spanish in advance than your get- away to Belize. You will in all likelihood say sure to keeping your mate's hand and taking a stroll after supper.

Intelligent Optimism

Scientists have, as of overdue determined that piece of the optimism we experience is careworn-in. It is genetic. This isn't always especially splendid, as a large portion of our attributes is genetic. Besides, it is smooth to appearance that some human beings are plenty greater fantastic and pleased than others. It seems to come lower back typically to them, and that is no uncertainty because they've got plenty steadily inherent (genetic) optimism. In any case, this will be an trouble for a few. Because of this careworn-in detail, scientists have determined that numerous people have unrealistically excessive requirements. They wish to be greater powerful than they become being, they desire to live longer than they do, and that they choice to be greater snug than they're - without putting a good deal exertion into it.

Does this mean we must be cautious approximately being excessively fantastic? Unquestionably not, however regardless we want to be cautious. We, as a whole, recognise that optimism is a suitable characteristic, and that positive people gain from a pair of factors of view. They have better well being, stay longer, and make more coins than cynical people. Thus, paying little thoughts to how optimism is obtained, it's miles as but vital to domesticate and enlarge it.

Furthermore, regardless of whether or not or no longer you do not have an entire lot of burdened-in optimism, you can, anyhow, determine out the manner to be a very advantageous character. Everything crucial is the proper technique and exercise.

What is optimism?

I'm positive that everybody has a definitely suitable concept of what optimism is. The word reference definition is "the choice that the ideal outcome will take vicinity." It's associated with trust. However, it's far now not the identical. On account of expectation, there's a part of self perception; you're wishing for some thing and function "self belief" it'll show up. Optimism is, manifestly, likewise related to the choice for a effective final results, but we are assured some problem will manifest due to the reality we agree with in ourselves. We understand we've got the stuff to carry out it.

How about we circulate now to what optimism have to not be. As a be counted quantity number of first importance, it should not be unrealistic. Wishing for something you genuinely apprehend you can in no way get does now not make a number of feel. (Obviously, it's miles constantly vital to bear in mind that lovely matters may be completed with sufficient tirelessness and guarantee.)

Reasonable optimism likewise is not the view that "everything is notable" and the whole lot will continually rise up ruddy. This is generally known as entire optimism, and it is something you ought to be cautious about. Try no longer to be idealistic to such an quantity that you're confident not some thing horrible will ever rise up. If you do, you might be in for a stun even because it takes vicinity. Life is brimming with issues, and also you should now not brush aside them. You ought to confront them head-on, and stay to inform the tale or acclimate to them, and generally remind your self that every one problems have arrangements; it's miles simply a query of locating them.

Intelligent Optimism

Along those traces, whole, unrealistic, optimism isn't always what you need to cultivate and broaden. What you genuinely need is "sensible optimism," and as we will see, the manner to it's far know-how. For smart optimism, a sensible mind-set is needed. Furthermore, this shows you have to begin with the aid of the use of the usage of identifying topics that you can not change and reputation on what you may trade or decorate. Besides, you have to be confident that regardless of whether a few factor unlucky takes place, you could famend it and determine out a manner to transport beyond it.

Intelligent optimism is a functionality, and like any functionality, it very well may be scholarly. Also, as specific skills, it requires a device of "experimentation." Try some issue - deliver it your the entirety - besides if it does no longer artwork, have a glide at some aspect one-of-a-kind.

At remaining, it's far important no longer genuinely to utilize the presence of mind and perception, but to likewise use your modern thoughts. Envision the final results of what you preference for - go through in thoughts it great. Envision the prizes you'll get, and the way you will experience. Play this time and again to your thoughts. Concentrate on it. This will gas your optimism.

Qualities of People with Intelligent Optimism

• They have a practical mindset closer to existence. They recognize that awful topics can take vicinity. However, they are confident they are capable of go with the flow past them.

• They are passionate about their future, but not unrealistic.

• They rise up toward the start of the day with the feeling that the day earlier can be a standout amongst others they've got ever professional.

• They famend topics - recognize that it is probably difficult to alternate brilliant subjects, however they don't surrender effectively.

• They make use of their records to inspire optimism.

• They remember misfortune to be transitory, and as a few aspect that can be survived.

• They believe in what they are doing.

• They reap that their very private high-quality is but to go back lower back.

• They seem upbeat and thrilled more regularly than now not.

• They famend what they've got.

• Procedures for Acquiring Intelligent Optimism

1.Keep in mind what you clearly want is sensible optimism - now not unrealistic optimism. But, maintain in thoughts your capacities and strengths.

2.Focus to your strengths, no longer your shortcomings.

three.Try not to stress over what you can not alternate. Focus on things you may alternate.

4.Gain from your mishaps and mistakes.

five.I choice to succeed.

Revelation of Optimization Practices

This week, we would like to speak approximately the project of optimization virtually as part of the do's and don'ts while improving. The under practices allude to upgrading computerized shopping for and selling strategies with a focal point on foreign exchange. While the under strategies may be connected to any mechanized device, the forex market and MetaTrader 4 is applied in the majority of our examples.

In rundown, optimization can be characterised as a technique that consequently well-known the maximum profitable contributions for a foreign exchange robot. For instance, foreign exchange robots can also have person expect earnings and prevent-loss parameters (for instance, TP = 50 and SL =

15). Utilizing the MetaTrader 4 platform, those parameters can be optimized to locate which values for assume profits and save you Loss might possibly return the maximum gain.

When walking an optimization, it's miles critical to take into account that the pinnacle settings decided with the useful resource of optimization are not constantly the incredible settings. Consider it, in case you run an optimization of taking profits, forestall loss, and shifting traditional incentive for all of 2009, the settings you discover are the pleasant settings for 2009! Markets are commonly showing signs and symptoms and signs of alternate and because of the reality you have got the pinnacle settings for consistent with week in the past, a month within the past, or a three hundred and sixty five days in the past, could no longer propose they will keep on appearing admirably on live marketplace records. What is optimization accurate for at that factor? Great question!

Optimization is a terrific beginning degree to discover some settings that have worked nicely previously and might preserve on working admirably in a while. For instance, we ought to accept as true with we ran an optimization of assuming profits and save you loss for 2009, and the pinnacle settings ended up being TP = a hundred and SL = 50. Since we recognize what the pinnacle settings were for 2009, how about we exercise the ones settings to 3 marketplace statistics outdoor of 2009; we want to then run a number one backtest using the ones settings on market records from 2008. This is gotten lower lower back to an out of pattern test due to the fact the data you're using the technique to is out of doors of the optimization pattern. If you directed a totally closing take a look at indoors 2009, it might be an excellent backtest due to the fact that is the length the strategy modified into optimized on.

After we discover our pinnacle pattern for 2009 and use it on out of sample market data (2008), we're able to make higher alternatives about our method. If the anticipate profits and save you lack of one hundred and 50 artwork wonders in 2008, splendid, we ought to clearly have a few aspect right here! This discloses to us that even in a single-of-a-type market situations, those parameter values held up; definitely encouraging find out! Then another time, if the technique bites the dust at the same time as you use it on awesome market facts, that must show to you the settings you are the usage of maximum probable won't hold up. Now, you will move again to the actual 2009 optimization, find out each other pair of parameters that worked properly, and supply them a shot 2008 (or any out of pattern statistics). The technique can be complicated, however optimization serves as an fantastic device for customers who information to utilize it. Below we are going to address more topics within the realm of optimization.

Over-optimization

This time period is applied reliably with "bend becoming." What takes place is that on the identical time as you over-optimize settings for a particular method (optimize right all the way down to every modest element), the quit end result is a momentous backtest for the optimization time body. This substances great thinking backtest and a remarkable price bend. Notwithstanding, at the equal time as you workout the ones parameters to a live account, the gadget quite frequently loses coins. You have fit the technique to at least one set of marketplace records, as we noted, that is a fundamental no-no. You want the set of parameters this is the most robust and exchanges well on an entire lot of market facts.

Walk Forward Optimization

Walk Forward Optimization is considered as the first-rate kind of optimization, and in spite of the fact that it's time-devouring, it locations any foreign exchange robot to a definitive take a look at. Inside walk ahead optimization, you begin through on foot an optimization for a specific time body, as an instance, how about we take optimization for all of 2008. After the optimization is finished, you acquire the maximum main settings and lead a again test with them on statistics that pursue the optimization window (2008). Because we optimized for 2008, we're going to take the top parameters and run a again take a look at for the primary four months of 2009 (we carried out the first 4 months because of the reality, for the walk-beforehand take a look at, you need to use a window one fourth the size of the optimization window). So once you check your method on the first 4 months of 2009, you can get a concept of approaches your system does on out of pattern records, short following an optimization. If your method does lovable, that is a amazing beginning, the subsequent step is to stroll the tool in advance and optimize for February of 2008 to January of 2009, and in a while lead a lower returned check for February of 2009 to May of 2009 and check out the out of sample searching for and selling. When you are completed, you are taking a gander at how your method finished at the out of sample assessments, if shopping for and selling is dependable, you can proceed onward to live statistics checking out, if it's miles powerless, you need to endure in mind a outstanding robotic or doubtlessly refining how you're using the parameters.

Most likely the above technique is lengthy and time expending, this is why we have deliberate our techniques for optimization called keep-optimization. This method includes directing an 18-month optimization at the present day day marketplace statistics (January 2009

June 2010) and in a while finding the top settings. When you've got got the precept 20-30 settings, you lower lower back check them in the course of a multi-365 days time frame (another time to 2000) and take a look at whether or not or not there are settings that change thoroughly extra than ten years. If you have a tool that transfers well in present day years, this is a few component that shows top notch guarantee, and you're most possibly organized for live demo checking out. Our method with keep- optimization is that the ultra-modern innovation, accrued expertise, and fee motion is restricted to the most current marketplace records. So, having an optimization on past due market records lets in you to locate the parameters which have held up within the present, and possibly from the begin (it genuinely is exposed through the multi-year again take a look at). Give it a shot; it is not as difficult as it seems.

I honestly sold a robot, presently what?

If you have got were given as of late supplied a forex robot and want to test it for maximum appropriate settings, we prescribe you begin through using taking a gander at the outside parameters of the robot. These are the subjects within the facts vicinity for the android, this means that in case you double-tap the robotic within the manual window and snap the statistics sources tab, you will see the rundown of outer parameters. These are the subjects that can be optimized; you want to recognize what they do in advance than you begin an optimization. More often than no longer, the subtleties of the parameters are covered into the manual for the forex robotic, and if they'll be not, we prescribe you contact the engineer to assist make bigger on what each putting does.

Important Life Connection

I am aware of no covered stable of definitive forces of the general public however the people themselves: and on the off danger that we suppose them now not illuminated sufficient to workout their control with a proper attentiveness, the remedy is not to take it from them but to endorse their carefulness. - Thomas Jefferson

Society consists of human beings such as you and me. We are operating units of mind, body, and spirit. Together, the three- manner association chooses and does our each day works. Accordingly, an mixture fact is created shared through the way.

The universe is generally displaying signs of alternate, and the entirety in the international influences the entirety else. People are not separate, but, running segments of an splendid entirety. The unit is on a par with the fellowship of its person. Each person holds importance within the impact of the group.

ONE BAND, ONE SOUND: Can you envision a society in which all people works at the best specific human restrict? Envisioning this is probably pretty a take a look at as it offers off a power of being outlandish. Have you heard the expression, "To alternate my disposition, you have to to begin with trade yours?"

Each capable grown-up is at final in rate of oneself. We have all that is predicted to streamline our important components. A negligible degree of time and interest have been given to the three vital components of our lives can appreciably make a distinction in any person. Only exchange influences the fantastic complete, no matter whether or no longer or no longer outstanding or bad. Positive modifications in an character will certainly modify the operating of the unit. Is it authentic that you are working searching after commercial enterprise employer?

MIND-BODY-SPIRIT CONNECTION

There is a three-course affiliation amongst thoughts, body, and spirit. Together they format the moments of our lives. The intuitive thoughts works inside the once more of the scene manifesting planted idea and conviction seeds, on the equal time as the cognizant mind interprets and reacts to encounters. Having the proper thoughts is in addition as important as having a healthful frame and a sustained spirit.

How is your thoughts? Is it vivid or complete? Does it count on nicely under strain? Is it versatile to change? Is it that you are organized to keep in mind matters and arrange as indicated by using brief significance? Would you be capable of create powerful materials for yourself and people round you? These are the whole thing the human mind is capable of.

Emotional sludge can slow highbrow capacities. Inordinate encounters of warfare or flight initiation now not just activate improvement of guarded power that could damage an invulnerable framework, it moreover motives beyond emotional reactions to times and occasions to stay dynamic and to unknowingly create modern comparative conditions. When this occurs, the mind cannot art work as in step with design due to dread and furthermore, anxiety.

Consider the person within the scenario below.

A multi-12 months elderly individual name Mildred and her husband of 25 years as of overdue separated. The essential component she feels she want to be appreciative for is the manner that theirchildren are presently each advanced and hitched with youngsters. She as quickly as loved this man. Presently she detests his guts!

Mildred is angry due to how she feels inside the wake of getting her ex obscenely uncovered with their close by neighbor. She found out the marriage would not closing the day they have been hitched after he coincidentally referred to as her an beside the factor name. Presently she feels moronic for intending with the provider and giving him her everything in some unspecified time in the future of her nightfall years.

Mildred's ex and father are only alike. Both talked to her like she have become vain. Indeed, she is damaged, as indicated with the resource of her convictions.

If she had any well really worth, her husband could not have undermined her, and her dad have to have loved her. She fizzled at pleasurable both. These are the contemplations which can be flowing in Mildred's heart and thoughts.

In the wake of sitting inside the four dividers of her studio condo irately thinking once more approximately the existence she as quickly as lived in a five-room domestic wherein she and her ex added up their children, Mildred takes her tote from the kitchen bar, and keys from the divider installation key-holder and heads to the community bar. Perhaps she'll find out some extraordinary guy who will love her superior to some thing her dad and ex. She wipes away tears, locations on her exercise face, and recognizes her existence. Genuine affection right here she comes.

OK, u . S . A . Mildred's thoughts is going for walks at effective nice running? Why or why now not? In mild of the statistics given in the state of affairs, do you obtain she can locate what she is looking for?

I'm positive, if we're straightforward with ourselves, you and I both have had moments in our lives in which our minds worked ineffectively. Emotional sludge is simply one reason at the back of a weary spirit. It is the handiest I will popularity on in this monetary disaster.

There is a marvelous chemical which could clean irksome sludge and reestablish highbrow capacities. Love is an emotional sludge chemical. It is capable of preserving apart obstinate discernments and convictions that maintain the thoughts complete and crippled. It will display fact covered up under messy lies and discover why pessimism is immoderate.

The undefeated stain expelling depth of love will clean any place of human lifestyles that it is related to; mind, body, and spirit. Purging feelings with love can also have highbrow wheels turning with smart power. In this mind-set, new ability effects are opened.

The human thoughts works great when practiced and enlightened. There are a greater huge amount of techniques than I can rundown to perform this. Working riddles, math problems, and gambling intellectual drawing in video video games can animate and make more potent highbrow preparing. Perusing books, magazines, and the usage of the internet or found out reproduction are first rate techniques to acquaint your thoughts with illuminating facts. An enlightening mind is one that is engaged.

Harmony is important for highbrow readability. Contemplation, hand handy fighting, unwinding song, and being ingenious are approaches to outfit proper serenity. Fuse an movement into your life that encourages highbrow clearness. To create a spotless clean mind is to have a glad one!

With a vibrant, really energized thoughts, you may deal with the body and spirit. If you resemble most Americans, you think about your body at any charge as speedy as each day for a few purpose. The hefty mindfulness has a few people fixated on their frame thinking they may be excessively speedy, while ones omitted inside the exposure be given they'll be too skinny. My sister, who is 5' eight", allows she is overly tall on the equal time as my multi-one year-antique little lady, who is 4', grumbles approximately being excessively quick.

My guidance for building up and maintaining up a wholesome body: Eat suitable additives of proper healthful nourishments, take first-class nutrients and upgrades and drink hundreds of water. This is the first-class diet for all of us kind. Address your doctor in advance than starting new systems.

I moreover endorse regularly on foot, no matter whether or not only a few short put off in an afternoon. Your cardiovascular framework will thanks with exquisite operating. Make top notch to position on supportive footwear as a way to strong your lower legs and knees. Characterize focused on muscle bunches with brief fiery workouts. Most importantly, deliberately envision yourself displaying your top of the line frame type, often. Act in self assure and entire conviction that you can accomplish your longing.

We have talked about intellectual and frame walking in the three phase affiliation. For reasons unknown, in this society, the territory of spirit is a touchy venture for some. Having a healthy spirit is vital to talk human prosperity generally, so I locate it essential to speak approximately in this financial ruin. Spiritual establishments effect each one-of-a-kind place of man or woman existence. A notable spirit offers properly being.

You had been created with love from love with the motive to like. It's a given; love is essential to have a slight, glad spirit. Open your coronary heart and mind within the path of every day interactions with special human beings. Begin to perceive the nearness of love at the same time as delivered; however in the course of a captivating enjoy at the grocery save. The cognizance of affection reinforces the capability to particular love. Love permits you to be close by of the maker. This is the region spirit generally feels unfastened.

When your thoughts is obvious, the frame feels great, and spirit is happy you take care of corporation. Different topics won't be as you want them to be. However, you are in a state of affairs to create with accuracy. Your needs are a beneficial concept away. Deal on the aspect of your whole self; thoughts, body, and spirit to get underway effective trade in order to usually enhance you to hid statures. Your power vibrations will resound into the universe and mirror self. I count on that you replicate thought.

CHAPTER 10: Personal Development Through Positive Self-Motivation

Self-Motivation in a pleasing manner is an internal strength that drives optimism out without hesitation for triumphing in life. Winners are pushed via desire! A winner will need to beautify upon their very very very very own improvement. There changed into no longer a consistent winner in any walk of lifestyles, who did now not want to win disguised. Winners recognize that the critical behavioral axiom in lifestyles is the fact which you and I do bypass inside the course of turning into our opinion of maximum. You and I are persuaded every day and moved via our currently winning issues. As such, we bypass in reality inside the route of that what we harp on.

Everyone in life is self-persuaded, a hint bit or a first rate deal, certainly or contrarily, even a preference to do not anything is a desire counting on notion. Inspiration is a energy which moves us to hobby, and it springs from in the character. Motivation is characterised as a sturdy cause faraway from or towards an item or circumstance, and it very well can be created and discovered, it'd no longer want to be feature.

Positive Self-Motivation Puts You in The Driver's Seat of Your Life

Anybody wishing to enhance upon their private improvement desires to with the useful resource of some way touch off their motivation. For a long term, it's miles been wrongly anticipated that motivation is extraneous, that it very well may be siphoned in from the outdoor via upward thrust up and circulate talks, or demanding situations or encourages. Such sports sports do deliver mind in training, useful resource, and motivation for people to expose on their innovative powers, yet virtually within the occasion that they need to and in reality if disguised.

That is the mystery; enduring trade is affected in reality whilst the need for trade is each comprehended and disguised. Until the reward or motivator has been hindered and disguised, it has no motivational energy through any way. So, the genuine champs in life are the individuals who have created, because of a widespread body of thoughts of first-rate self-choice, or optimism, a sturdy exquisite self-motivation. This is a key to enhancing your very very private development.

At the quit of the day they built up this potential to transport within the course of objectives that they set, or jobs they need to play, and they may persevere via nearly no diversion from transferring inside the route of these goals. In the face of all discouragement, missteps, and misfortunes, this inner stress maintains them transferring upward inside the route of self-satisfaction. Motivation is an emotional u . S . A ., and the excellent bodily and intellectual motivators in life, as an instance, survival, starvation, thirst, retribution, and love are altogether accused of feeling.

Thekey emotions which overwhelm all human proposal with inverse; but, nearly same outcomes are fear and choice.

Fear is the maximum robust cynical helper of all; fear is the exquisite compiler and the immoderate inhibitor, fear confines, fixes and frenzies, forces and at last leaves plans and annihilations goals. Fear can pulverize someone's personal development and inhibit any try and decorate it. Desire conversely resembles a robust superb magnet; reaches opens, coordinates and it attracts in and energizes, and accomplishes dreams.

Fear and desire are posts separated, and they purpose replacement fates in lifestyles, fear generally seems to the past, and desire appears to what is to go back lower back. Fear vividly replays common evaluations of failure, discomfort, dissatisfaction, and disagreeableness and is a hounded reminder that similar reviews are probable going to rehash themselves. Desire but triggers a reminiscence of pleasure and fulfillment, and it energizes the need to replay those and to make new triumphing evaluations. The devouring jail phrases of the fearsome man or woman are probable going to be, I want to, I cannot, I see hazard, and I preference. Be that as it may, preference says I want to, I can, I see an possibility, and I will. Want is that passionate nation among in which you are and in which you want to be. To have a success personal development, we want to discern out a manner to manipulate fear genuinely as with preference.

In life, winners apprehend that their presently overwhelming contemplations will control the majority in their movements and that you can not harp on the transfer of a idea. That is why you can not get in shape in case you maintain thinking about how fats you'll be; you can't quit smoking if you find out your self to be a smoker and similarly you can't get rich in case you are pressured over your payments. Winners take into account the hazard to be an opportunity, they see the rewards of success earlier, and that they do not see the punishments of failure. They enjoy personal to be as a terrific step inside the path of a superior existence. People crushed thru dread can't act with preference or decisive purpose; they experience life reacting in defensive.

It's an unusual and calming fact that the element we worry most, we supply to skip. Deep gaining knowledge of is the right intellectual anecdote, for fear, and distress. Desire sparks interest which consumes immoderate adrenaline in the framework. It continues the thoughts occupied and the expectancy of accomplishment alive. High achievers in lifestyles have solid self-development abilities, and they keep a excessive diploma of concept. The struggling power that moves them to motion originates from inner their selves. Success in existence isn't always saved for the couple of; success is reliant upon energy and backbone.

We need to research and keep in mind how to build up this winning movement nature of notable self-motivation. It's critical that allows you to recall that everyone is self-inspired, both a bit bit or a extremely good deal, sincerely or adversely and that motivation isn't always discretionary, even the choice to do not anything is a motivation. Our fears or our dreams persuade each one human beings. Anxiety is unavoidable due to the fact it may get you out of risk and spare your existence, it may preserve a children's lifestyles, but as a addiction or a lifestyle, fear has an amazingly unstable reaction.

Fear is a pink mild that could save you unstable behavior, however preference is the inexperienced moderate that releases you beforehand towards your desires. So your maximum precious exercise in developing first rate self-motivation is to try to supplant fear motivation with preference motivation. Luckily, because of the fact fear and choice aresides of a similar coin, this is not as hard because it seems, through all money owed, to be.

Fear of poverty can be supplanted with a need for affluence.

Fear of ache may be can be supplanted with a desire for right nicely being; dread of unhappiness can be modified with a ardour for success. Every the sort of actions need to be present to accomplish progressed non-public improvement. A lack of try is equal to giving in; even as there can be no actual try to look for improvement, there may be no improvement at all to experience over. Try no longer to provide the worry of failure a threat to give up you to your adventure for additonal huge private improvement, keep onto the selection for entire fulfillment and actual-life pleasure. Winners realise that their presently triumphing concept spurs them, so your attention need to be on the praise of the achievement which you search for, in area of the practicable punishment of failure. Make preference your presently overwhelming concept, and it will compel you with the motivating energy for success in all factors of your every day life.

Behind each winner is a deep yearning of optimism and enthusiasm in the route of the praise of success and not the punishment of failure, close to the association in preference to the troubles and in the direction of the appropriate reaction in preference to the inquiry. Behind every winner are the passionate longing, simply the need, and the infinite stress for complete stepped forward personal development.

To Follow are Some Action Reminders Towards Positive Self- Motivation!

For one aspect, supplant the phrase cannot cope with can within the everyday jargon, can observe to approximately ninety 5% of the problems you revel in.

Next, supplant "strive" with "will," for your each day jargon, that may be a type of semantics and builds up your new mentality of residing on subjects you may do virtually than on items you need to try with that integrated excuse earlier for workable failure. Focus all of your strength and hobby at the fulfillment of the goal you are engaged with the winning 2nd; dismiss the results of failure. Keep your pressure for private development on the main edge of your thoughts.

Failure is only a transitory exchange in course to type you out on your subsequent fulfillment. Remember, you generally get what you bear in mind maximum. Next, make a rundown of your 5 maximum urgent dreams or goals, and ideal along each, positioned down what the result or advantage is on the equal time as you accomplish it. See this rundown earlier than you head to sleep every night time and after waking every morning. Always supply arrangement placed enter at the equal time as human beings disclose to you their problems. When the troubles are your non-public, recognition on the short concept..."What's the correct reaction?" Seek out and communicate with a person this week this is presently doing what it is you want to do maximum, and make sure that it is someone who's doing it properly. This applies to a few issue, acquiring, or promoting, snowboarding, or performing, speaking, overseeing, or however being an outstanding companion or determine.

Find a expert, get the facts, make a project of getting the maintain close of the entirety you could approximately specific winners in the subject.

Enroll in a class to test it, get personal sports activities, and bring fervor thru manner of mentally staring at yourself getting a charge out of the achievement. At final, make it a addiction for every one in every of your dreams, to rehash, and all once more, "I want to, I can, I need to, I can." The electricity the ones steps will have at the improvement of your private development is immeasurable. You will experience empowered, fortified, and a success; nothing can stop you, your achievements will heap one upon each other, you'll comprehend what real non-public development seems like in real existence.

How To Change Your Life For The Better

Change is an inescapable factor which has an first rate sensational effect on our lifestyles. Each new day is an possibility to exchange our lifestyles for the better. Varieties embody us, and there can be no evading exchange because it will locate us, venture us, and strength us to rethink how we inventory on with our existence.

Feeling down channels your power, expectation, and force, making it tough to do what you need for a advanced life. Be that as it may, you can not keep away from trade because of the reality the extra you oppose it, the extra tough your existence turns into.

It has this uncanny functionality to arise to hurry with you at the same time as it's far the least predicted and can make an uneasy feeling or an upbeat one on your existence. At those moments, you are regarded with deciding on a choice or being pressured to do it.

Transforming yourself for a advanced one is not a fast or clean fix. However, it is some trouble but an great accomplishment. Unpredicted circumstances are likewise not some element you can awaken from. However, you could have greater energy than you understand.

Know the Process of Your Mind

You have to recognize that your cognizant getting geared up mind goes at one hundred miles for each hour round your cerebrum at the identical time as your oblivious managing goes spherical a hundred,000 miles for every hour spherical it. It is the form of high-quality accomplishment; wouldn't it now not no longer say it isn't?

In this manner, it implies that your conscious is best a spectator to what your oblivious directs as it is the only making each one of the options earlier than you even concept of you make a decision. Regardless you do now not agree with me?

An ongoing disclosure uncovers that your unconscious mind regularly predicts the selection or the reaction you have got been going to make, as long as seven seconds earlier than your conscious mind knows approximately what's going on.So, at the same time as you could take shipping of as real with which you have quite in recent times settled on a preference, seven seconds in advance than that, your oblivious has without a doubt taken a gander at all the alternatives and made the selection you made.

What may additionally need to you be able to do? The secret is to apprehend which you have a time edge of seven seconds.

Alistair Horscroft, an Australian speaker, recognized for his TV association "The Life Guru," has the response to these seven seconds and made a video about it.

Change is a Catch-22

Change resembles a Catch-22! It requires movement; however, taking movement even as you're hit or harm is not easy.

Change, for the maximum element, emerges for your existence due to a preference or an emergency, or with the aid of manner of some coincidence. It isn't smooth, surely at the same time as you come back to find out your self at a miserable spot. It is then which you need to look the way to adjust your element of view to supply you decrease decrease returned up.

Since conditions or issues to your lifestyles appear excluded; they thump you wobbly with a sense of perplexity, every now and then in dread, and go away you injured, every now and then profoundly.

You can't keep a strategic distance from startling occasions from taking region, manipulate them, or understand why you're encountering such sorting out moments. In any case, you could select a manner to react to them. Your picks are what are empowering you to make adjustments to decorate topics or now not.

What pursues are a few tips on the maximum gifted technique to change your lifestyles, step by step, to discover your self adapting higher to unanticipated events and instances that emerge.

Keep Your Dreams Alive

When troubles hit us, we incline to tug lower returned and separate. It regularly feels an increasing number of beneficial to withdraw into our shell. Instead, set apart that try to understand what is crucial to your existence.

Concentrate in your goals. Consider what makes you thrilled. By preserving your dreams alive, it will provide you with a purpose and capability to have a look at a compass at the super way to make the adjustments you want to maintain on with a superior life. If you do no longer, you may spend the the relaxation of your lifestyles drifting thru it absurdly without any dreams, way, middle, or purpose.

You want to likewise apprehend that social assistance is crucial to what befalls you. Find methods, of all styles and sizes, to assist specific human beings by attractive within the humanitarian try, be a listening ear for a companion in trouble, spend time with a creature or accomplish some component tremendous for any person.

Make a Vision Board

As a teen, you familiar that something became possible. You could wander away in myth land constantly. You have been proficient at imagining and envisioning what you may be while you grew up.

We, as a whole, lose that capability as we form into adulthood. Your problems and mind get blanketed up thru the obligations you get, and also you begin to forget approximately or take shipping of that undertaking your desires is unbelievable.

Making a Vision Board is an amazing impetus at the way to begin attaining and confiding for your goals all once more and imagining your wishes every day on a vision board will breathe lifestyles into high fine modifications. We, at that factor, begin to accept as true with inside the probability of making them training session as predicted.

Be Positive

You can not constrain yourself to have some properly instances or revel in delight, but you may strain your self to do certain subjects, regardless of whether or not you do not enjoy find it irresistible.

Regardless of whether or now not trade does not depart away straight away, you will chew via the usage of bit feel higher and increasingly enthusiastic to make time to pay attention on preparations in vicinity of troubles.

Practice contemplation. It can assist decrease sadness, decrease the pressure you have were given amassed, and lift high-quality emotions, happiness, and prosperity. Reward your self with moments of satisfaction and well known and show appreciation as soon as an afternoon.

It is one of the ways to change your lifestyles for the higher. You ought not to overlook a few splendid moments because of the truth you're too bustling concentrating for your problems raised thru trade.

Set Goals

When your fancy lifestyles seems alive yet again, you need to make a set and circulate prolonged-haul, non permanent goals and medium. It is following up on those targets that empower you to perform a alternate to enhance matters.

Keep in mind your existence might also additionally trade as events appear suddenly. However, you need to typically be adaptable in improving your sails with the breeze that blows and bear in mind these adjustments.

The little advances which you are creating a flow into for alternate to get up for your life.

Experience Knowledge

When you revel in or advantage a few new beneficial know-how, you beautify your know-how and with it come greater reality. It makes you often flexible and adaptable to precise occasions on your existence.

Accordingly, thru escaping your regular type of familiarity, you get little by little o.K. With the tough to apprehend.

Perusing books is an extremely good course with a view to have a look at. You should in no manner end looking and getting more understanding because it offers your life that means and to exchange your existence, it is useful.

Try no longer to Have Regrets

You should understand that regrets are events of the past and in case you spend it gradual brooding about it, you may bypass over wonderful matters in the present as what is to go back returned isn't always however composed.

You recognize you cannot exchange what you probably did or didn't do in beyond times, so permit it circulate. The essential aspect you have got control over is how you maintain on at the side of your gift and future existence.

Here is a honest technique to take away regrets: Get a few inflatables and explode them. At that component, compose on each one in every of them a trouble you lamented and later on allow them to go as you phrase them going off into the sky, bid farewell to the ones regrets for eternity.

Deal with Your Fears

If you need to exchange your lifestyles for better, you need to determine out the manner to rule your feelings of dread so they can not have manage over you anymore. They are definitely musings you area for your thoughts which are not right; you in fact accumulate that they'll be legitimate.

You should understand that it's miles your apprehensions in life that save you you from sporting on at the side of your existence without limit. Be that as it could, at the identical time as you face your emotions of dread, you reclaim your ability to pick out out and pick out the way you need to carry on together along with your lifestyles and whilst to do this, you do change your existence for eternity.

You have to make a rundown of stressful topics which you could sort of need to do but are excessively hesitant to. Set up an association and make a circulate to do them.

Think Differently

Try now not to sum up your lousy encounters. Think as an alternative, "I can do something I positioned my thoughts to."

Try not to look subjects in darkish or white. Think rather, "I fizzled, but subsequent time I might not."

Try no longer to reduce the superb of a situation. Think as an possibility "She stated as an entire lot, and I take into account it."

Notice each one of the topics that went right in choice to the subjects that grew to emerge as out badly.

Try now not to shape a hasty opinion via making fake understandings with out proper evidence.

Try no longer to just accept that the way you revel in right currently displays truth. Think as a substitute, "I recognize I am a victor!"

Never, underneath any instances, call yourself inadequately. State instead, "I'm headed, and I am justified, no matter all the hassle!"

Try now not to maintain yourself to what you want to and ought not to do.

To close to, you want to recognise that the number one person who is going to make a change for your existence is you and simply you. So now, I depart you with a preference to make, on the way you want to trade your lifestyles for better. If you're making a flow on my message, stop ifs, ands or buts out of your mind-set and change your life until the prevent of time.

Change Your Life By Visualizing

When human beings are keen on growing a noteworthy existence exchange, it very well can be alarming. Most of the population is impervious to exchange due to the fact they examine the distinction with torment. I'm going to impart to you an extremely good adventure to be able to alternate that obvious torment, into the direct inverse - a few element that makes you revel in top notch.

It's referred to as visualizing.

Visualizing the way you want to stay is one of the first-class techniques to seriously trade your existence.

If you are new to this exercise, I'll provide you with a word forthright you may also experience marginally awkward from the start. We're introduced up in reality as we apprehend it turned into visualizing, or wandering off in myth land, or fantasizing approximately what we need is usually disliked. How frequently need to you be able to consider wandering off in fantasy land in college, and the educator guided you to wake up and interest?

In any case, what is so misconstrued approximately visualizing is that it receives you to where you want to be. The children that were found wandering off in fantasy land in elegance are comparable children which is probably presently sporting on with the lifestyles they longed for every this kind of years decrease decrease lower back.

Our minds are robust. Each time we interact an concept in our mind, it sends our body into the concerning vibration, and, sooner or later, we observe up on that vibration. Fundamentally, our mind manipulate our feelings, and our emotions dictate our movements. If you query this, take a gander on the monetary unrest that any such huge big style of humans are encountering in recent times. They have permitted thoughts of lack and constraint to dictate how they're feeling - misplaced, bewildered, and terrified. Since they are in this bad vibration, they act in strategies that guarantee extra loss of their existence. They reduce decrease again on their expenses. They keep themselves in an profession they may be miserable doing. They cannot see an exit plan because their truth is in reality sincerely one in all lack.

If they have been no longer feeling such dread, they may never yet again be restrained. If they located out that the whole universe become truly to be had, they may recognize that they may be liable for all additives of their lifestyles. They would not worry the monetary gadget or stay in an profession they detest. They might possibly recognise that lone they manipulate their lifestyles - no longer anyone or some aspect else. They might apprehend that they control their very very own bills, and that they manipulate their pride. So they may expect plenteous, satisfied, existence-giving thoughts, which cause them to enjoy those fantastic feelings, and they act in exceptional approaches that decorate their lifestyles.

Have you at any element visible that you think in images? If we don't forget some thing, an photograph is predicted in our thoughts, and we are capable of see that concept. Think approximately the automobile you pressure, the kitchen you're making your dinners in, or the mattress where you hit the hay. Think about inner a cinema, retaining up in line at the air terminal, or going to a football wholesome-up. In a everyday development, those snap shots fly into your mind - you could see each one in each of these objects.

So, due to the fact we assume in photos, it allows us to bridle this power of visualizing. We can genuinely snap the photograph we discover in our mind and redecorate it into the physical shape in our reality.

Choosing what you need is significant. It want to be easy. Generally, this workout may not offer you with awesome effects. You likely might not get any consequences. You should genuinely plunk down and make feel of what you need from existence and the manner you need to live - all factors of it. From the form of house you need to the sort of mate you need, within the form of footwear you will placed on, to the each day life-style you may lead - take a few minutes and file the whole thing. The greater detail you located into this picture of your new lifestyles, the better your consequences is probably.

Since you've got got an low cost image of the sort of existence you want to live, in all its grand wonder, you need to devour this photo into your mind. So, near your eyes, and start to visualize the image you definitely recorded.

It is critical to do this unfiltered. I do not get your which means by means of manner of the use of unfiltered? Indeed, think a few part of your new existence makes them possess some thing large, you'll ponder internally, "I declare a quite smooth and current a few element. I love the use of it down the roadway in complete extravagance and pleasure as I feel its strength flood in a few unspecified time within the destiny of me." That is the manner you need to count on even as you visualize the existence that you want.

The separated version of this idea is probably some issue along the traces of, "One day I can also furthermore claim that pretty high-priced a few component that I have no clue how I will endure."

Do you see the difference? In the two times, you're placing your feelings into the picture - that is vital to this exercising. In any case, you want to make a contribution genuinely incredible emotions, now not bad ones.

The unfiltered idea is your choice in its maximum top notch structure, at the equal time as, the sifted concept is your desire with limitations. If you start isolating your desires, the photo you're visualizing will in no way display up due to the reality you could make a contribution terrible emotions and visualizing the lack in preference to specializing in electricity and abundance. So, recognize if you start to do this and save you it from gaining out of electricity. Remember, you're in control of your lifestyles.

To visualize correctly, you have to be separated from each person else together along with your thoughts. There isn't always any arranging this. So, execute all distractions - your cellphone, the tv, the sound device, the PC - some thing on the way to make your mind meander. You may additionally want to determine on not to conflict to pay interest what the universe is trying to present you.

As you don't forget your new existence, revel in the entirety approximately it. Feel the first-class. Feel the affection. Feel your self being content fabric material with the entirety for your life. If you need a circle of relatives, be content material material material how glad you are that you have a family. If you want to preserve your very private commercial agency, experience the explicit pleasure because of the truth you could win your very private cash, time allowing, challenge a few thing you want to do.

Numerous people visualize themselves BECOMING this character they want to be - and that is a hundred% off base. If you believe your self attending to be, you'll always be manifesting a condition of getting to be. You need to simply accept as real with as in spite of the truth which you

136

are as of now that man or woman and right now carrying on with that existence due to the truth that is the element if you want to transport into the structure. Remember whilst you had been a baby, and also you imagined you have got were given been a global-magnificence competitor or a well-known artist? This is the equal.

You'll need to do that exercising for a few minutes in any occasion as soon as each day -instances if you can. You cannot take transport of the electricity that you may launch when you begin to visualize your new existence frequently.

To recap, first, you ought to characterize what you want. At that aspect, visualize someplace in which you're undisturbed, and in reality experience your natural, unfiltered preference of this new life. When you're carried out, you can experience your frame in a vibration of strength and pleasure. It is this vibration as a manner to dictate what you do, and the results you can get. By visualizing frequently, you may alternate your existence quicker, and more comfortable than you can have ever predicted.

Use A Sick Day To Change Your Life

Sick days are a bit of lifestyles. You can permit yourself to be overpowered with disappointment, reprimand yourself for the entirety you may not whole, and fear each muscle because the minute's cruise through using. You can likewise employ the day to invigorate yourself, to lighten up your tired body, and to change your lifestyles. Your reaction to contamination involves a selection if you could part of the bargain and compelled, or active and content. Here are ten approaches to make a sick day green and profitable. In what manner will your next unwell day change your lifestyles?

Create a first-rate frame of mind. Did you understand that quality, enthusiastic states and sound strain the executives can help your insusceptibility? An research thru the University of Wisconsin-Madison (Davidson 2004) recommends individuals who react with pleasant feelings have unique mind motion produced with the resource of those feelings that expands insusceptibility. Following up from unique investigations that show the frame of mind can have an effect on your health, this unique exam preferred to apprehend why. The scientists anticipated antibodies created inside the wake of accepting an influenza immunization and determined an growth within the resistant response for the individuals who had a outstanding complete of feeling fashion. React to existence certainly, and you will be greater healthful. How would possibly you deal with the strain of unhappiness or the unexpected? Make high-quality you have what it takes to compartmentalize your emotions and placed everything into element of view. When you are ill, you need to enable your body to fight. Make sure you win the combat in mind.

You may be more healthful if your mind thinks valuable and uplifting musings. When you are sick in bed isn't always the time to consider each one of the stuff you cannot do. Instead, set up with your self to ponder what you CAN do.

As crucial as you're in your commitments, deliver yourself consent to be human. This does not advise that you drop the whole thing each time there may be any trace of a sniffle, but don't be on the alternative awesome, directing place of business paintings at the same time as being triaged at a clinic. Life is a careful workout in careful manipulate. Live it with a passion that starts offevolved with a extra fit body of mind.

1.Offer your self a reprieve. Your frame wishes rest even as you're sick. Sustain it and get invigorated. Treat yourself to the gentlest tissue you may discover to your sore nostril. Get the most agreeable pads and covers, and locate your chosen spot to curve up and rest. Enable others to think about you, and be thankful when you have cherished ones spherical to assist. Unplug your self from the world. When you are immensely throbbing and requiring rest, turn off your phones, and tremendous far off devices. If you want to keep one on for crises, push aside it besides if it is a true catastrophe (clue: visitor identity).

2.Revise your wishes. Think about the rundown of stresses or undertakings whirling spherical on your thoughts, and after that, do this intellectual exercise. If you had been to kick the bucket this actual right away, what might also in any case don't forget? Whatever is presently unimportant may be do away with until day after today. Quit thinking about it now. For the ones errands which is probably as but crucial for the afternoon, delegate them right away. Complete the exhibits early and after that, determine to brush aside them. If you are concerned approximately the very last outcomes, positioned individuals you believe liable for dealing with everything you have got special with the intention that they could do the stressing. Presently unwind.

3.Fight it. Be resolved to conquer it as rapid as time lets in. If you can't physically rise up, you can, anyways, reap first-rate subjects collectively with your mind. Choose to make the day clearly considered one of achievement. When you are eager, in desire to eating in bed, sit down in which you typically eat. A alternate of room can help bring a regularly nice point of view. After you start to revel in exceedingly rested, scrub down.

4.Utilize the time your frame is resting to take an character stock. It is better to talk approximately this which you are content material material together along with your lifestyles? Is it accurate to mention that some component is disturbing you? Are there any areas for self-hobby and development? Is it actual which you are viably coping with your pressure and a while, or can also you have the ability to utilize a few higher-adapting aptitudes for higher success? Is your life seminar at the proper track? Pick 3 topics, and choose to accumulate your boldness and create a superior you via confronting them. Did you recognize that many maintain in mind burnout to be a hollow amongst your desires and your praise (Farber 1983)? What do you anticipate that isn't happy? As you start feeling higher, plan a few issue to project out. It also can unique some being worried phrases to any man or woman. It can be starting a diary to allow you to evolve to life. You may want to probably want to peruse a fantastic ebook or peruse the net for studies and reachable hints. You can also moreover get the fearlessness to begin a agency, follow for each different function, or go back to beauty.

5.Assess your otherworldly existence. Is it clean to say that you are content cloth with your self inside the lonely instances, or does the calm reason disrupting feelings to ground? Is it easy to say that you are effective approximately your convictions about God and your affiliation with Him, or is vulnerability developing inconvenience? Supplicate, observe the Bible, or tune in. Spend a

6.a part of your loosening up day being a console to your spirit thru the author of solace. If you expel the existence of God in your lifestyles idea, utilize this time to consider if you are taking the defects of others and crediting them to God. He isn't always the author of your torment, however He is the person that can assist you to get out of it. I regard you reserve the selection to differ with me that God exists; but, ensure which you are terrific approximately your choices.

7.Stay on course. Try now not in charge your contamination for being wrecked out of your way in existence. If you have got been eating nicely, at that element, maintain doing it. Because you may consume crackers for some time does no longer suggest you have to make up for all of the misplaced suppers after you sense like ingesting all another time. When you're better, live privy to the responsibilities you made previously. If you avoid delicate sugars (as a person does), at that thing affably disclose to the good-natured partners, who us of a you want Jell-o or Gatorade which you are doing remarkable and dandy at any charge. There is sans sugar Jell-o in case you should have it, with every one of the synthetics that involves. If you keep away from liquor, at that point, do not take Nyquil (which has 10% liquor). There are loads of virus drugs handy if function remedies are not your inclination.

I pursue an ingesting plan which has helped me live in recuperation from my consuming problem for greater than 14 years now. It includes consuming adjusted sustenances approximately every 4-5 hours and keeping in mind that there are adaptability and collection, she has a base and maximum severe she want to flavor for each placing. This liberates me and encourages me deliberately abstain from putting my emotions into nourishment.

When she become unwell and incapable to eat, that doesn't advise she modified into off my plan. She will now not be wrecked. Here is one stunt she makes use of that may permit you to recognize if you are endeavoring to veer off base. If she become simply ready to eat crackers from the begin, at that detail, so be it. She famous while she starts offevolved to experience higher, she may additionally furthermore contemplate internally "well, she as yet unwell, so she may want to feel unfastened to devour a whole package deal deal of crackers because of the fact it'd consolation/unwinding/a laugh, and stress over adjusting it later." This is a warning for me, and he or she or he fast realizes that if she wants to justify it, and employ an emotive phrase ("comforting,..."), at that aspect she became ok to consume better. She won't be organized to devour a serving of combined veggies, yet she might be able to simply add some different dietary training to my dinner. Furthermore, when ill, protein is fantastic for assisting the body re-advantage electricity.

What is it you justify inside the wake of being unwell? It is easy to say which you are thinking about stopping your hobby device simply due to the reality you had to pass over a day? Is it solid to say which you have been persuaded on the identical time as venture a few near the residence reason, and could you say you are presently enticed to toss it apart? Fight to live on the right track and prop up to your voyage. You are justified, irrespective of all the problem!

1.Start any other addiction or destroy a terrible one. Why sit down tight for New Year's goals? Utilize your sick day to start new. Have you idea about the influences of your crucial coffee? Besides the financial price of a delicious Starbuck's restore, there can be a real charge. You have maximum possibly officially encountered the caffeine withdrawal manifestations (low strength, cerebral pain, and so on) in some unspecified time in the future of your illness. Why bypass back? Push in advance. Have you favored to surrender cigarettes, and find out that your frame rejected them even as sick? Try no longer to boost them another time for enthusiastic motives; however, make the maximum your unwell day and begin a shopping for plan. Have you desired to start operating toward or eating better? Utilize the time to create a plan for whilst you experience higher. You might also moreover discover that feeling so lousy creates a few enthusiasm for the opportunity of feeling so nicely. Spur yourself and select at any rate one dependancy to interrupt or begin. At that issue, do it.

2.Dream. What can also you do if you may change your life? Utilize your ill day, a day trip of your run of the mill time desk, to undergo in thoughts your lifestyles path. Set targets and thing excessive. Prepare to stun the world. It will be very nicely; no character will giggle. Furthermore, no individual may also even recognize if you stay calm. Consider telling any character your dreams, goals, and desires. You may also find out consolations in amazing spots. At that issue, make a pass. Is it higher to mention that you are left with an all- encompassing infection? Think approximately how you could utilize the time to assist other humans. The maximum extraordinary malignant increase pledge drives begin with one character considering what to do to effect the area. Shouldn't a few detail be said approximately you?

three.Develop, create, and increase. Before your day is finished, beautify your lifestyles. Discover some new information. Watch a story or "a way to" appear on tv. Peruse a ebook approximately a topic you do no longer have the foggiest concept about. Peruse the net to recognise what you don't generally are looking for out. Assess your life reason, your percentage of fulfillment, and reflect onconsideration on your powerful attain. Create a put up on your weblog if you have one, or carry what desires be thru whatever medium your capacity permits. You may be extraordinarily beneficial on the same time as your body rests. You may also even exchange your life. Do it these days.

CHAPTER 11: Optimism is Good For You

What is optimism?

Optimism is an idea firmly diagnosed with happiness. It is ready not surrendering while times grow to be really difficult. However, at the same time as the going is ideal, having optimism implies you expect that the good want to continue. It is tied in with having an expectation, and generally accepting topics will enhance. Being an optimist places you in an super function to deal with conditions in your life and to cope with life's troubles for the maximum aspect.

As a rule:

Optimists accept awful subjects are quick. They from time to time arise (in area of typically) and might not ultimate. For instance, your supervisor yelling at you on Monday does no longer recommend they will yell at you for the relaxation of your strolling lifestyles. An optimist has a mindfulness that lousy topics will get up in life. However, they are capable of rise up all over again at the same time as the terrible takes place. It implies they are able to anticipate responsibility for his or her life, instead of choosing not to trouble, as what is the reality, it's miles the entirety going to reveal out terrible anyways.

Bad activities aren't their shortcoming. For example, the horrible weather situations made it difficult to win. It is straightforward guilty your self unreasonably. However, regular self-blame can harm your self assure if you may take a gander at outstanding reasons you generally generally tend to, which consist of yourself higher. You must be in rate of your movements; anyway, your reasoning have to be realistic. An optimist does now not surely blame themselves whilst some difficulty appears badly.

Optimists preserve horrific sports to that one particular situation. For example, because you not noted one birthday, does no longer cause them to neglectful in all factors in their lifestyles. You coincidentally forgot that one birthday. If awful matters occur, it isn't the a part of the association and might moreover be considered as problems to be triumph over. Optimists do now not overdramatize the scenario.

Interestingly:

Optimists count on that proper activities ought to last. For instance, heating the great cake - they do now not consider this to be a completely specific case. They are an excellent cake maker; as a result, their desserts are commonly right. Interestingly, while optimists succeed, they commonly tend to invest extra power subsequent time, therefore making fulfillment more likely.

Right activities are of their own making and are because of their capacities and inclinations. This mind-set can serve to make you experience appropriate approximately yourself. It manner taking a outstanding feature of chances after they emerge and having the fearlessness to risk — for example, having the courage to trap up a functionality vocation possibility, in preference to disregarding it and at very last passing up a super opportunity.

For optimists, appropriate subjects come to have an effect on one-of-a-kind regions in their life clearly. It improves all that they do considering they experience particular approximately themselves. For instance, achievement at artwork improves your mind-set to your private home lifestyles. They do now not u . S . A . They appear like a superb bookkeeper (and they're now not hundreds that properly, it's far clearly no person else wants to carry out the obligation) however the relaxation of their lifestyles is a damage.

How is optimism tremendous?

Physical fitness

There are right nicely-being motivations to be superb. Research demonstrates optimists have extra grounded resistant frameworks, making them much less powerless to contamination and illness. They are a good deal much less willing to bite the dust of a coronary coronary coronary heart attack or cardiovascular infection. Other studies demonstrates that an wonderful mind-set implies you could get higher faster from an interest. Optimists have a lot much less strain, which averts many strain- related clinical problems, and it's miles proposed them at closing live more.

An interesting factor approximately optimists is that they're positive to discover a manner to live clean of illness and rush to get treatment whilst infection strikes.

Emotional properly-being

Optimism may be an top notch reality promoter for the motive that it may provide you with a sense of control on your existence. It can enhance your good sized prosperity. The studies did through manner of Seligman emphatically demonstrates that optimists have a great deal less despair. Optimism can prevent you feeling inclined, this is an important purpose of distress. Optimists were proved to be steadily a hit in all normal issues, together with art work, sports sports activities, and connections.

How optimism can assist?

Optimism is a mind-set. It is in reality the contemplations you country as quickly as a day even as you experience particular situations. Your musings can amazingly have an effect for your existence. Thinking hopefully empowers you to take pleasure within the right subjects and overcome the wrong stuff. In that functionality, it gives you the critical concept to perform your objectives, each large and little. Odds are you can collect extra, as an positive mind-set will provide you with the stress to keep onward. After fulfillment, an optimist will invest extra power, ultimately prompting extra success. They do now not placed success proper proper down to karma, opportunity, or wonderful outer influences. It can definitely manual you without hesitation as you recognize the picks you have got have been given and the quantity you could do on the side of your life.

Optimism, similar to happiness, isn't always a few mystical wonder that maintains awful subjects from taking area. It does besides provide you with the hazard to come upon accurate stuff for a more incredible diploma of time and be in a state of affairs to deal with the lousy topics in a excellent, attractive way.

One could probably say that a part of negativity keeps us grounded, however optimism can flood us in advance. . They do now not placed achievement right all the way all the way down to karma, possibility, or other outer impacts. It can truely assist you without hesitation as you understand the choices you have got and the amount you can do together with your existence.

How to Succeed with the aid of the usage of Creating a Definite impact in Your Life

There is a massive variety of steps which may be important to reap fulfillment with the resource of way of developing a incredible change on your life. Our "present" is normally filled by way of using sincerely absolutely one in allsubjects. This is, we each regularly hold to the past, or we sit up for our destiny. While it is ideal to take note of the beyond, actually as to the destiny, we need to make every push to do as such in a pleasant and useful manner. Reflection and expectation are fruitful for us on the same time as we're:

"Taking the know-how of the beyond, making use of it to our gift, with an surrender purpose to make a a success and worthwhile destiny"

In this guide, you'll be familiar with the way to be successful with regards to growing a remarkable exchange in your existence. You will figure out a manner to appearance the beyond as a notable gathering of information, practice that information in the "now," and make your very very personal clever stop cease end result for the destiny. If you have got were given were given mentioned that a change ought to be made, and you're equipped to start authorizing that trade for your lifestyles, you want to keep perusing. If you haven't stated that a change need to be made, and you're organized to move... All matters taken into consideration, no vicinity. You need to quit perusing right away right right here and grapple with the way that stagnation isn't always something above a rearing pit for disappointment.

Desire

To acquire on the subject of developing a change in our lives, it's miles important to want to trade. That is to say, and also you need to have a honest choice. If you are changing due to the fact you decide it will make every other person guide of you more, or such as you greater, you have to avoid another time as masses as that "stagnation" spill. You can in no way really CHANGE besides if YOU need the exchange, and have a authentic desire for it. If the concept of trade is frequently close to home and critical to you, you're very at risk of be an increasing number of diligent in seeking out after it. It is additionally important to guarantee that you don't forget the "benefits and downsides" of the trade which you want to make on your existence before taking off on the adventure to attain it.

Capacity

Presently, as you middle across the exchange which you want to attain to your lifestyles, you want to consider your capacity to perform the transformation. As it have been, is the exchange that you want to make sensibly speaking? If it is not reasonably talking, you could discover your self beaten with whole and particular dissatisfaction. It is concept and perceptive that there can be a sure degree of "fact" that need to be confronted on the subject of alternate. We as a whole love the ones outwardly engaging forms of adjustments that make us sense all exceptional and gung ho, but in all truth, there are a few adjustments which is probably affordable and a few on the way to bring about everyday dissatisfaction due to the way that they will be now not inner our capability.

Positive Thinking

Indeed, I am going to expose to you that the depth of extremely good thinking will make you a success in terms of creating a change to your lifestyles. I recognize, I recognize... You have heard the whole lot formerly. Wouldn't you're saying there may be some diploma of legitimacy to this recommendation if it's so "fashionable"? Honestly, you want to preserve your musings straight away almost about accomplishing change. How might also additionally you are making a alternate and agree with in it if you constantly anticipate that you cannot? Did you ever stop and recollect if you are thinking that you can't say which you are the number one character conserving you over from all that you may involvement in existence? If no longer, you want to think about this. Stay first rate, and you're in all likelihood going to be very a achievement!

Patience and Support

Patience and help areof the primary fundamentals with reference to triumphing with a alternate to your life. To begin with, you need to decide out how to build up a hint endurance for the transition to show up. We as a whole, listen, "trade does now not get up in a unmarried day." I do not recognize precisely how a brilliant deal fact there may be in that assertion because of the reality I do get hold of that trade can occur in a unmarried day. It won't be the massive aim which you have your factors of interest set on. However, definitely the choice to make a alternate is a alternate - what did that take you, all of five minutes if that? The secret is being understanding even as it goes to the ultimate results. We should don't forget it... Not very many "artful stop result" had been made in an afternoon. Aren't you a magnum opus? Obviously! We as a whole are! Take as an lousy lot time as critical and get the lines, the shapes, and the sun shades proper. You may be glad that you did!

Support is some different vital element in phrases of growing a alternate on your lifestyles. There is a big shape of styles of beneficial aid that you could come upon while looking for to make a change. The secret's to "preserve in mind new ideas." How about we see, loved ones are top notch manual frameworks. Expert advising and schooling property are superb, as properly! Enjoy one, experience all! You soak up as an awful lot assist as you can. Keep in mind, the team that has the maximum players is frequently the organization that leads the % in any real undertaking. Amazing a group - a group a first-rate way to assist you to win even as growing a change for your life!

Positive Psychology What it's miles and How to Use It?

In the high-quality 'antique days, psychology changed into for the maximum element approximately research. They had to see how reflexes worked (touch warm stove... Ouch! Permit your hand be moved away), commentary worked (I see an older grownup... Presently I see a princess...) and the way behavior labored (hound sees nourishment... It salivates). When psychology began, it had 3 factors: deal with and join intellectual sickness, aid 'innovative genius' or wonders which in the ones days may additionally had been pressured with intellectual contamination, and assist each day human beings live better lives.

The highbrow illness changed right into a mainstream aspect after WWII and WWI. Psychologists who play in labs and allow addresses in some unspecified time in the future of the day had new vocation openings. They might also need to cope with the ones who've been returning home from battle stricken by intellectual contamination. What's more, poof... A ton of financing and coins-filled reading the manner to repair what wasn't right with people. Well in 2008, we presently realize A LOT approximately what's up with human beings. We have medicines for optimum mental ailments or maybe a few fixes. We furthermore apprehend a high-quality deal about revolutionary genius; but, in popular, psychology did now not realise a ton approximately your always. Joe Seligman went through the bulk of his time on earth studying melancholy and tested that depression is placed out. At that factor he asked, should not a few factor be said about exceptional religion? For a long term, psychologists believed that during case you took an individual who have become discouraged and removed their melancholy, you will have a happy man or woman. However, that isn't valid. Because you do now not have a cold, may now not suggest you're ideally strong.

Because you are not discouraged should not recommend you experience energetic, euphoric and love your life. The place of excessive high-quality psychology sometimes alluded to because the observe of happiness uses the equivalent clinical meticulousness that has been associated with studying what goes on with humans and the way to restoration them, to statistics the broadness of human functionality.

Positive psychologists lead research on things like self warranty, versatility, coarseness, take delivery of as genuine with, bliss, amazement, tendencies, happiness, movement, supplication, and silliness. Anybody can exercise the studies that has left super psychology into their lives and vocations. Specialists, as an example, psychologists, advisors and life mentors, employ advantageous psychology to discover what is as of now working with customers and help them accumulate their features, discover willpower and significance of their life.

They assist them experience happier and gradually satisfied. Positive psychology is unique than "fortunately." We are not supporting humans to be happy, happy, satisfied continuously. It's vital to revel in irritated, upset, and dismal whilst it's far suitable.

That is emotion every one of the emotions that human creatures count on in choice to trying to reveal to ourselves we have to be satisfied continuously. It's tied in with allowing your self to sense all remarkably up with out stalling out. For a long time, psychology did now not authorize human beings to be human. The problem emerge as intensely slanted on highbrow illness; extraordinary psychology is tied in with night time day trip the size.

Bringing as loads interest to the fantastic aspect of existence as we need to the bad. The studies leaving tremendous psychology is charming. At no extraordinary time have researchers ran twofold daze fake treatment ponders on such things as happiness, appreciation, and right religion. Presently, you may think, why attempt directing a research pay attention to discover that doing accurate topics for others can permit you to experience better? I concur with you. Innately we apprehend the ones topics are pinnacle and we need to do that. Be that as it can, what number of hopeless or marginally sad humans do you run over to your existence? What type of people do you apprehend that make a unique try to perform some issue first rate for some different individual?

Far advanced, make a unique effort for a whole outsider? Research suggests that you may significantly and quick decorate your happiness degree clearly via engaging in a few factor decent for every other individual. These human beings are happier, have better connections, are regularly cherished via others, and feel better approximately themselves. Indeed, we understand that doing this stuff can income our lives. Be that as it can, we overlook about. Or however, we do not understand the impact it is able to have on us. Sound scientific research is fantastic stuff. An exam confirmed that earnings reps who examine abilties on carrying out more potent and hopeful were three times more powerful than their discouraged companions.

If you are an organization proprietor, that may be a notable ordeal. Research shows that taking factor in paintings that empowers you to make use of your dispositions and what you're generally well at empowers you to be happier in addition to step by step feasible. Makes sense, right? However, what numerous human beings do you recognize that get the possibility to do what they'll be unique at and prefer to do each day? Positive psychology is splendid from self-improvement and dad psychology.

Its organizer Martin Seligman is assured that first-rate psychology want to be spellbinding, in preference to prescriptive. Which approach, rather than getting to know what expands happiness and in some time telling human beings a manner to govern their lives, high-quality psychology want to portray the research on those factors. As in keeping with Seligman, humans lead sound investigations on additives, for instance, flexibility, appreciation, and petition, make sense of the manner these items effect people and the additives through which they paintings.

At that issue, they educate people what the studies suggests. For example, thinks about display that talking builds your experience of exquisite emotions and reduces the issue results of depression. Appreciative humans are often idealistic about destiny activities, revel in increasingly more related to others, or maybe record higher best relaxation. As researchers direct those examinations, they plan to apprehend the components associated with appreciation: how can it work? Why does it paintings?

Positive analyst nation, "display human beings the research, assist them make educated alternatives approximately what may also art work exceptional of their existence." This is ground-breaking and notably extremely good from endorsing or telling humans a manner to live their lives.

As a high great psychology-based existence mentor, I consolidate every an exciting and a prescriptive technique. I painting high-quality psychology- based absolutely strategies for making the remarkable alternate clients need to look, and I make tips depending on what has worked for me and others.

As a subject, remarkable psychology has taken off. Simply Google "happiness" + "observe" and take a gander at how plenty happiness has been in the media as of late. Attempt phrases like flexibility, euphoria, humor, traits, coarseness, existence satisfaction, and you could see that immoderate exceptional psychology is rapid extending. The formal which means of terrific psychology, a l.A. Wikipedia, is "the scientific research of the capabilities and ethics that empower people and networks to flourish." Every month there may be an ever-developing range of charming examinations turning out in the subject. We have scarcely started out to expose what we understand to be the ones traits and ideals; in any case, fantastic psychology is changing people's lives round the area.

If we aren't developing we are deteriorating

If we are not growing, we are weakening.It is human intuition to maintain developing, retain studying to maintain improving. We have no acquaintance with the entirety. We, as a whole, have physical sports activities to study. I'm speculating which you would love to decorate your existence because of the fact you're perusing this, or possibly you want to trade the whole thing about your revel in. If your situation is at that factor, do not give up because of the fact there can be a 'thump on' effect.

When you convert your reasoning, and you exchange one problem for your existence, then the whole lot else will follow.:-) Maybe it's miles your hobby you want to trade, or your price range, your dating, weight, self-notion, well-being or likely the entirety seems super but some factor is lacking, however you can't understand why you are as but ?

The problem is we revel in life harping on what we are discontent with, grumble approximately the ones things and permit them to make us substantially regularly hopeless. Every so frequently we can also additionally try to take care of them, but we lose middle, and it would now not maintain going surprisingly lengthy (at any point made a New Year's Resolution?)and then we beat ourselves up for 'growing brief,' and the cycle begins offevolved.

There are certain matters we need to keep in mind in advance than we're able to change. There are likewise subjects we need to do after we've got made Strides One. These preliminaryranges are highly normal motives we flop so nowsubsequent time you may be positive.

Stage One

Choose WHAT you need! Who may additionally need to you need to be? How ought to you need to sense? (Truly, its a selection, you may feel it now if you decide to) What do you want to do? Where ought to you want to move?

Be unique. Consider it cautiously, write it down and take a look at it every morning and each night time. This will hold you centered.

When you observe it enjoy the feelings, you'll have in case you as of now have it, press the passion and the pride, and the appreciation.

Stage 2

Make a Decision, a right a hundred% dedication! Not, oh, I need I had that. Make a assure to your self, a pledge, that is the detail that I will do, and I can do it! The most vital piece of that is you FEEL appropriate. Feeling terrible approximately your problem/state of affairs or your self will make you experience more lousy and the problem greater regrettable. (See The Secret Explained). Begin to feel engaged and extremely good, excited, and certain determined, and happy.

You benefit it; you will do it!

Be benevolent to yourself, your claim closest partner. Feeling accountable makes you hopeless, and the component right here is to feel top. Lose the blame stop beating yourself for not being perfect and highlight on all that is ideal approximately you and your objective. Enormous your self up! Harp on your traits and the topics you need about yourself. If you cannot reflect onconsideration on any you really need to try this, ask a cherished one what they love approximately you but, please try to do it independent from anyone else first.

Keep in mind how tremendous you are; that is why you ARE loved and cope with your self as goals are. Alright, so now you've got decided on what you need and made a willpower to your self that you could accomplish it.

Stage 3

Accept. If there can be a query for your mind, then you definitely definately definately need to put off it fast as this demonstrates disappointment is as however a desire, and it isn't always.

Our very very very own ideals are common from begin; they are instilled into us by using manner of way of our parents, circle of relatives, friends, and encounters and make our notion of ourselves. They have an effect on our mind, our feelings, our goals, and our relationships and the manner we enjoy about ourselves. We will have exquisite beliefs and beliefs that maintain us down on what we actually can do. Our beliefs can supply us a roof that we be given we cannot get via.

They set out models for ourselves in our lives. They direct what we revel in we advantage and prefer this what we accomplish. Do you observed there is any wealthy individual who coincidentally made their cash? No, they standard they deserved it and have been eager to widely recognized no a lot much less, that doesn't propose their ideals/requirements are as excessive in unique elements in their lives, as an example, relationships, fitness and so forth.

Our beliefs set our measures; we need to be for the purpose that we DESERVE what we're searching for to have, that we're right sufficient, that we are able to do it. We make motives to ourselves regarding why we can't have it/do it. This stems from our beliefs (and fear, but we're going to get to that some exceptional time).

There is no reality, just perception. What's greater, your notion is your conviction, and you may exchange your beliefs if you decide to, and after that, so change your 'existence.'

Things being what they're, How Do I Change My Beliefs?

Well, our lengthy haul imbued beliefs are set up in our unconscious thoughts, we aren't thru manner of any approach aware of a big portion of them. However, I

182

believe that nowapproximately this, you may begin to understand your very private issue restricting beliefs, and afterward, you could most in all likelihood change them.

You may additionally recognize that you rehash specific examples for your lifestyles, in any area, in all likelihood in relationships or with cash. These examples originate from poor ideals we have have been given, and you can don't forget them with the useful resource of brooding about any tedious behavior you can have. It is probably near home relationships; do you watched again and experience as although your final couple of relationships were as even though you went out with a similar person over and over?

Or as an alternative, do you preserve gaining money but in no way seem to have any? Plunk down and document any restricting ideals or examples you could understand and file why you can have created them.

This might be a clumsy workout; however, it's miles justified, regardless of all of the hassle as if you have identified them, you can supplant them with new powerful ones. They are essentially terrible thoughts we have were given approximately ourselves and our lives, but, like I said before they might emerge out of our subconscious, so we need to construct our interest to what we are in fact thinking.

Stage four

Changing your poor ideals is the maximum dominant method to exchange your existence. Regardless of whether you recollect you could or you would now not, you're capable of most in all likelihood right.